The Problem of Original Sin in American Presbyterian Theology

by George P. Hutchinson

sola fide
PUBLISHERS
www.solafidepublishers.com

The Problem of Original Sin in
American Presbyterian Theology
by George P. Hutchinson

Second Edition
Copyright © 1972, 2014
by Linda Hutchinson

Published by Sola Fide Publishers
Post Office Box 2027 Toccoa, Georgia 30577
www.solafidepublishers.com

Cover and Interior by Magnolia Graphic Design
www.magnoliagraphicdesign.com

ISBN-13: 978-0692240618
ISBN-10: 0692240616

To Paul Woolley

Professor of Church History
Westminster Theological Seminary

in gratitude for his concern
and counsel through the years

Table of Contents

Foreword
by John Murray

The theology of one generation can never be divorced from historical antecedents. This is true whether the theology espoused is radically divergent from that of the past or progressively and constructively in agreement with it. When divergent its character can be assessed only in terms of that from which it is divergent. And, if there is agreement, the foundations of the past continue to be those of the present. This is but to indicate how indispensable to theological study is historical theology.

The present publication is a study in historical theology, restricted as the title indicates, in both theme and scene. It should be understood at the outset that Mr. Hutchinson does not bring within the scope of his research the whole doctrine of original sin in American Presbyterian theology. He focuses attention on one all-important aspect, namely, the nature of racial solidarity in Adam and of the sin entailed for mankind by reason of this solidarity. This concentration of interest is warranted by the direction given to the debate within American Presbyterianism, and no apology is necessary for confining the discussion to this subject.

Mr. Hutchinson has done a great service by setting forth in lucid terms the viewpoints of the leading protagonists in the dispute, particularly from the time of Jonathan Edwards to the present. In the judgment of the present writer, the space devoted to J. H. Thornwell, R. J. Breckenridge, R.W. Landis, and R.L. Dabney is of special value; it fills what has been a conspicuous blank in historical presentation and assessment.

In the concluding chapter pertinent and searching questions are posed. They suggest the lines along which further developments of the doctrine should proceed. It may be relevant to propose that a more guarded analysis of the term "imputation" as it applies to the involvement of the race in the first sin of Adam would relieve the question of some of the difficulties that have harassed theologians. It is hoped the publication of this dissertation will promote not only better understanding of the history pertaining to its subject but appreciation of the basic relevance of that which is discussed. The reality of Adam as the first man, of his sin as that which brought sin and death into the world, and of the sin of all in Adam's sin undergirds the Christian faith. Some of the complexities of the historical debate may perplex rather than edify many sincere students of theology. But the encumbrances that often accompanied the controversy should never be allowed to obscure the fundamental issues bound up with Adam and his sin. Mr. Hutchinson's study is a vindication of the jealousy which theologians of the past entertained with respect to these issues.

Bonar Bridge, Scotland
September 30, 1971

Preface

The following historical study is presented to the public with a view to furthering a rising interest in Reformed theology among evangelical Christians in the English-speaking world. It is hoped that, in these days when this precious heritage is so sadly neglected, this effort will make some small contribution toward a renewed interest in it.

The study itself is substantially, with only slight alterations, the typescript submitted in 1968 to the Faculty of Westminster Theological Seminary in partial fulfilment of the requirements for the degree of Master of Systematic Theology. Thus the level of research in the introductory chapter (where I have depended to some degree on older secondary sources) is not as profound as it might otherwise be. This is one reason why the thought of publication did not occur to me until it was suggested some time ago by Professor John Murray (see Foreword). Meanwhile, the pressure of other pursuits has precluded any further work on the subject, other than attempting to improve the mode of expression here and there. There is also another reason why I have hesitated to allow this study to go into print, and that is that I had hoped to be able to incorporate it into a larger book including a more detailed history of the discussion of the problem of original sin up to and including the New England theology, as well as some attempt to deal with the problem myself. But this book probably will be a long time in coming! And the following pages will, without these envisioned contributions, confront the reader with both a self-contained study of an episode in the history of theology which has received no attention elsewhere, and a serious attempt to analyze the issues involved in one of the most difficult of all theological problems. Had I the opportunity to recast the study, there would no doubt be certain changes. For instance, I would expand the chapter on the Princeton School with a more detailed exposition of Charles Hodge and a more substantial discussion of the contribution of A.A. Hodge than that which occurs at the beginning of the chapter on the Westminster School.

Finally, I would like to take this opportunity to thank the Faculty of Westminster Theological Seminary — especially Professors John Murray (emeritus) and Paul Woolley (see Dedication) — for their contribution to this study; and Mr. Charles H. Craig of the Presbyterian and Reformed Publishing Company for his interest in it. May the Lord be pleased to prosper all our efforts to glorify His Holy Name.

George P. Hutchinson
Goethestrasse 24
Tübingen, Germany

Introduction
The Problem and Its Background

The essential importance of the doctrine of sin to the health and progress of the Christian religion on earth is evident to all who will soberly reflect upon the implications of its denial or perversion. For the supreme interest of Christian teaching is salvation, the salvation of sinners from sin. Consequently, the character of the salvation which is in Christ can never be properly comprehended apart from the sin which is in the sons of Adam. This truism is especially pertinent with respect to that aspect of the doctrine which has been traditionally characterized as the doctrine of original sin.[1]

Now Christian men have ever been struck by the awesomeness of that doctrine of original sin delivered to them in the holy scriptures. It is a momentous enough fact that all men are sinners, in that they have sinned and fall short of the glory of God, with all the attendant evils which the presence of sin among men entails. But when the apostle explicitly traces the origin of that sinful estate back to the first transgression of the first man Adam, the effect is breathtaking: "Through one man sin entered into the world, and death through sin. By the trespass of the one the many died. The judgment came of one unto condemnation. By the trespass of the one, death reigned through the one. Through one trespass the judgment came unto all men to condemnation.

---

1. Cf. the statement in G. P. Fisher, *Discussions in Theology*, "The Augustinian and the Federal Theories of Original Sin Compared," New York, 1880, p. 355: "The one word which expresses both the nature and the end or aim of Christianity, is redemption. The correlate of redemption is sin. Parallel, therefore, in importance with the doctrine of redemption in the Christian system is the doctrine of sin. The two doctrines, like the facts which they represent, are mutually inseparable..... The disease must be known and admitted before you can comprehend the remedy," etc.

Through the one man's disobedience the many were made sinners."[2]

Nevertheless the wonder produced in men's minds by this doctrine has not precluded the asking of many questions. For the doctrine of original sin has over the centuries raised problems in the minds of many, Christian and non-Christian alike. These difficulties cluster around three problem areas: first, the nature of sin and the sinner; second, the nature of Adam's first sin; and, third, the nature of that connection between Adam and his posterity, which makes their sin traceable back to his. With respect to the first problem area, such questions arise as the following: What is sin anyway? In what exactly does it consist? What is essential to it? What is the relationship between sin as an act and sin as an attitude? What is the precise character of that sinful condition in which men find themselves, indeed, into which they are ushered at birth? What is the nature of its guilt and corruption?

With respect to the second problem area, the major questions are: What really happened when Adam sinned? What was the precise nature of his first sin? In what did it consist? In what ways did it differ from all other sin, both his and posterity's? How was it possible for a holy man to sin? What was the character of the temptation which induced such a man to plunge himself and his descendants into such unspeakable miseries?

The questions raised within the third problem area are: How is the first sin of Adam the origin of sin in the human race? What is the relationship between the one original sin of Adam and the original sin of all descended from him? What is the relationship which all men sustain to Adam so as to render his first sin in some way the origin of sin in them? How is it possible that his sin should be transmitted to his posterity? In other words, the question, in the words of the eminent Scottish theologian William Cunningham, concerns "the right mode of explaining the bearing of Adam's first sin upon the character and condition of his posterity."[3]

But the questions have not only been raised concerning the possibility of the existence of original sin, but also concerning the possibility of justifying its existence. In other words, how can original sin, assuming

---

2. Rom. 5:12, 15-19. All quotations from scripture, unless otherwise noted, are from the *American Standard Version*, New York, 1901.

3. William Cunningham, *Historical Theology*, Vol. I, London. 1960, p. 507.

there is such a thing, be reconciled to the canons of justice, whether human or divine? Non-Christians have for the most part maintained that such a doctrine cannot be reconciled to any ordinary human notion of justice; while Christians have had considerable difficulty reconciling the doctrine with the justice of the God of the Bible. The difficulties of relating the doctrine of original sin to the justice of God correspond to the problem areas mentioned above. First, how is it possible to reconcile the condition of original sin to the justice of God? How is it right for men to be born in a sinful condition which they cannot help or alter, a condition which renders them liable to the eternal condemnation of God? How is it possible to justify the *condition* into which all men are providentially born?

Second, given the origin of the original sin of the race in the first sin of Adam, how is it possible to reconcile such with the justice of God? If God foreknew that Adam's first sin would plunge his progeny into a state of sin, why did He allow him to sin? Why did not Almighty God prevent the introduction of sin into the human race from the start? Just what relation did He sustain to that fateful event? In the light of His power and goodness, how can one justify the *origin* of original sin?

Third, how is it possible to justify that connection between Adam and the race, and thus between his sin and their sin, which renders his sin the certain origin of their sinfulness? How can the human race, taken corporately or individually, be made responsible for what Adam did long ago? How can that fateful *connection* which indeed holds them responsible be reconciled to that justice which is indeed the expression and the glory of the character of God?

It is the purpose of this study to discuss how the third of these problem areas has been handled in American Presbyterian theology. It is obvious, however, that all these problems are closely interrelated. For the questions relating to the nature of sin and the sinner cannot be divorced from those relating to the nature of the first sin of Adam. And both sets of questions are comprehended in the general question as to the nature of the connection between Adam and his posterity through which all men are sinners by way of his first sin. It is on this very account that this particular problem may be called *the* problem of original sin. Nevertheless, despite the comprehensive relations of this particular problem with which we are dealing, we shall make every attempt in our study to limit discussion to it — that is, in summary, the problem of how we should understand and justify the existence and rightness of whatever relationship does in fact exist between Adam and the race. In other words, the question: What is our relationship to Adam? How is such a relationship possible? Given its possibility, how is it just?

Nowhere in the history of theology has this question been given more serious attention than among Reformed theologians in America, especially among the Presbyterians. The spirit with which they have treated the subject is exemplified by the comment of one of them when he calls it "a matter which penetrates into the lowest depths of human consciousness, which lays hold of the highest interests of the soul. which has agitated the most devout minds, and elicited the most earnest and anxious thoughts of the profoundest thinkers for eighteen centuries."[4]

This comment also evinces the fact that the American Presbyterian theologians did not start *de novo* in their attempt to formulate and defend the doctrine of original sin. Behind them lay a long history of discussion which confronted them both as an occasion for embarrassment and as an arsenal of strength. It is necessary at this point to review the high points of that discussion in order to sketch in the theological inheritance of American Presbyterianism with respect to the doctrine of original sin, particularly as it relates to the specific problem with which we are dealing.

The ancient church rejected as unscriptural the solution of Origen, inspired by Platonic philosophy, that the souls of all men voluntarily sinned in an ante-mundane state of pre-existence. After all, does not the scripture plainly state that the origin of sin in the race occurred with the sin of the first man Adam? In accord with this basic conviction, there have arisen within the church some six approaches to the problem of explaining the nature of the connection between the sin of Adam and the sin of the race.

First, there is the *Pelagian* approach which denies that all men are born in a sinful state of corruption and condemnation, or guilt. Rather all are born in the same state of moral neutrality in which, it is supposed, Adam found himself before the Fall. Adam's sin of course injured the race, but only in the sense that Adam set a bad example for all to imitate. According to Pelagius, "It is said we sinned in Adam, not be-

---

4. J.H. Thornwell, *Collected Writings* (ed. J.B. Adger), Vol. I (Theological), Richmond, 1871, pp. 518 f.

cause sin is innate, but because it comes by imitation."[5] Thus Adam's sin has affected his descendants, not by any natural process of propagation, but by the power of his evil example to effect the voluntary imitation of his sin. Any other explanation impugns the justice of God. For if God is just, He cannot create men in a sinful state any more than He can condemn any man for the sin of another. "It cannot by any means be conceded," says Pelagius, "that God who remits to a man his own sins, should impute to him another's."[6] Such notions could not be scriptural since they are obvious contradictions of "self-evident reason."[7] Moreover, its adherents maintain that the Pelagian doctrine alone comports with the scriptural parallelism between Adam and Christ. For just as Adam is only a bad example for us, so Christ is our Savior, according to the Pelagian teaching, only in the sense that He is a good example for those who desire to imitate Him.

Second, there is the *Augustinian* approach. Contrary to the Pelagians, Augustine taught that according to the scriptures sin is innate in man. All men are born with a sinful nature in a state of corruption and guilt due to the propagation of this sinful nature from Adam by the process of natural generation. This innate sin is *original* sin as distinct from the *actual* sins committed by men. Original sin passes from Adam to all men since in him all sinned in common previous to any personal sins which may accrue to them as individuals. When Adam sinned the race sinned. Human nature sinned in him so as to constitute a generic sin; so that the sin was not only Adam's own personal sin, but the sin of the

---

5. Quoted by Augustine, *De nature et gratia* (x). This rendering is from W. G. T. Shedd, *History of Christian Doctrine*, Vol. II, New York, 1892, p. 95. It should be noted that while Pelagius himself accepted the traditional Latin understanding that Romans 5:12 explicitly teaches that all sinned in Adam (ἐφ ᾧ πάντες ἥμαρον), his disciple Julian of Eclenum adopted the translation widely received in modern times, namely, "in that all sinned" (cf. American Standard Version).

6. Quoted in Augustine, *Anti-Pelagian Writings* (Nicene and Post-Nicene Fathers, ed. P. Schaff, Vol. V) , New York, 1887, p. 70, from *De peccatorum meritis et remissione* (III, iii). It is obvious that the Pelagian position assumes a strong creationist doctrine with respect to the origin of the soul.

7. According to the Pelagian Julian of Eclenum, the apostle Paul could not have taught that all have sinned through Adam, "lest he be believed to have taught something against self-evident reason." Augustine, *Contra secundam Juliani responsionem imperfectum opus*, II, 53; *"ne quid docuisse contra rationem perspicuam crederetur;"* in J.P. Migne (ed.), *Patrologiae Latinae*, Tom. 45, pp. 1164 f.

whole race, the Adamic sin. Thus the whole race is chargeable with the guilt of Adam's sin, or more precisely, of the Adamic sin.[8]

But how did the race sin in Adam? The Augustinian answer is simply, "In Adam all sinned, as all were that one man."[9] All were identical with him in that nature with which he was endowed with the capacity to generate them. But what is the mode of their identity with him? The answer is an appeal to the scriptural notion of a seminal union existing between ancestor and progeny. Just as Levi may be said to have paid tithes in the loins of Abraham, so we all may be said to have sinned in the loins of Adam.[10] It is on the basis of this seminal union of nature that the sin of Adam can be justly imputed to his posterity, as not the sin of another but as their own; though it may be called the sin of another in the sense that at the time it was committed, the individuals of the race had not come into personal existence.[11]

To the Pelagian charge that the justice of God is vitiated by this doctrine of original sin, Augustine replies that it alone explains why infants, who have committed no actual sins, are born into a state of suffering and mortality. For such penal evils could not be inflicted upon them by a just God were there not a just basis for doing so, namely, original sin. Moreover, original sin is voluntary in that it originated in the evil will of the race having voluntarily sinned in the Adamic sin. As such it is justly deserving of the wrath of God.

---

8. Cf. G.F. Wiggers, *Augustinism and Pelagianism* (tr. R Emerson), Andover, 1840, p. 273. Cf. Shedd, *op. cit.*, p. 81: "To be guilty of Adam's sin, in the Latin anthropology, meant to be guilty of the *Adamic* sin." For discussion of the Augustinian anthropology, see the standard histories of doctrine. For a discussion of the history of the doctrine of original sin to the end of the eleventh century, see J. Gross, *Geschichte des Erbsündendogmas* (2 vols.), Basel, 1960, 1963.

9. *Ibid.*, p. 278. See *Anti-Pelagian Writings*, p. 19 (*De peccatorum meritis*, I, x).

10. The specific scriptural reference is to Hebrews 7:9 f. The following quotation neatly sums up the Augustinian doctrine: "God the author of nature, but not of sin, created man upright, but he having through his own will become depraved and condemned propagated depraved and condemned offspring. For we were all in that one man, since we were all that one man who lapsed into sin.... The particular form in which we were to live as individuals had not been created and assigned to us man by man, but that seminal nature was in existence from which we were all to be propagated." *De civitate Dei* (XIII, xiv) as rendered by Shedd, *op. cit.*, pp. 76 f. Cf. J.N.D. Kelly, *Early Christian Doctrines*, New York, 1960, p. 364.

11. *Anti-Pelagian Writings*, p. 74 (*De peccatorum meritis*, III, viii) .

Then also it is maintained, that this doctrine, rather than the Pelagian, is sustained by the scriptural parallelism between Adam and Christ. For as men become righteous through a new birth in Christ, just so they become sinners through their old birth in Adam. As by a natural generation they contract original guilt and corruption, so by a spiritual regeneration their original guilt is remitted, though original corruption is not removed until the resurrection.

Whereas the Augustinian doctrine was well-received, indeed refined, by the philosophical Realists among the Scholastic theologians,[12] philosophical Nominalism led to a distinctive *Nominalist* approach to the matter of the relationship between the sin of Adam and the sin of the race. Briefly, the Nominalist doctrine is as follows: Original sin consists solely in the liability of punishment (*reatus pœnæ*) for the sin of Adam. William of Occam defines it as "the guilt of a foreign sin without any inherent demerit of our own" (*reatus alieni peccati sine alique vitio hærente in nobis*). Thus men are born subject to the punishment of Adam's sin but without any inherent depravity of nature. The Nominalists, while admitting that men are born in a state of moral degradation on the sole judicial ground of Adam's first sin, refused to call this degradation truly and properly sin since it is not the result of volitional activity. We could not have really sinned in Adam because we were not there to do so. Therefore, we are simply regarded as having done so though we are not *really* guilty, but only *nominally* so.

This Nominalist doctrine was presented to the Council of Trent by Ambrosius Catharinus, who maintained that the transmission of sin from Adam to his posterity cannot be explained on the basis of any natural relationship between them since the corrupted condition which

---

12. It is to be noted that we do not mean that these theologians accepted all aspects of the Augustinian doctrine of original sin, but simply that, with respect to the particular problem with which we are dealing, they followed generally in the footsteps of Augustine, attempting to refine his doctrine with the tools afforded them by philosophical Realism. For a discussion of the problem from an Augustinian viewpoint see Anselm's *De conceptu virginali et originali peccato* (analysis in Shedd, *op. cit.*, pp. 117 ff.) and Thomas Aquinas, *Summa Theologica*, Ia, IIae, 81, 2. Here we note that Thomas, in illustration of the Augustinian solution, appeals to the analogous union among members of a political unity. This idea of union between Adam and his descendants whereby they are considered judicially one was later taken up by the Nominalists, and especially by the exponents of the Federal view of the union which gained much prominence in Reformed theology.

is passed on through natural generation is not really sinful. Therefore, must there not be some legal relationship by which this transmission can be adequately explained? To answer his own query, the Romish divine suggested that sin is transmitted by virtue of a covenant, or pact, between God and Adam's descendants similar to the divine covenant with Abraham and his descendants. Upon the terms of this covenant, Adam's first sin is imputed to his seed in the sense that they are legally chargeable and punishable for it.[13]

Calvin and the Reformers, Zwingli excepted, strongly withstood the Nominalist doctrine on Augustinian ground. But curiously enough, with the rise of the *Federal* theology, the notion of a covenant between God and Adam was to become the distinctive mark of the classical Reformed doctrine of original sin.

The exponents of the Federal theology reasoned from the long-established notion of a covenant of grace back to the existence of a covenant of works, or nature (*fœdus naturæ*), made between God and Adam in the Garden. According to its terms God promised Adam eternal life if he should, within a certain period of trial, perfectly obey the divine precepts; on the other hand, disobedience brought with it the realization of the threat of eternal death. The issue of this trial involved not only Adam himself but all of his posterity since he was constituted their federal head; so that when Adam transgressed the covenant, all men transgressed it with him and thus became liable to undergo its promised penalty.[14]

---

13. This discussion of the Nominalist approach follows R. W. Landis, *The Doctrine of Original Sin*, Richmond, 1884, pp. 391 ff. Unfortunately, Landis does not carefully document his sources, and readily available literature on the Nominalist doctrine of original sin is scarce.

14. It should be noted that for the covenant theologians this concept of a covenant of works was not the product of speculation nor merely of natural theology, but firmly embedded in scripture. For instance P. Van Mastricht appeals, first, to Hos. 6:7 and Job 31:33. Then he refers us to the discussion of the apostle in Gal. (e.g., 4:24 ff.), where we see that the covenant of works was re-enacted in the covenant of Sinai. Next, what about the synonyms for the covenant of works in the New Testament, for example, the principle of works mentioned in Rom. 3:27 and the expression "under law" in 6:14? He then affirms that all the essential ideas of such a covenant are in Gen. 2, and finally appeals to their congruence with the other great heads of Christian doctrine. Heinrich Heppe. *Reformed Dogmatics* (tr. G.T. Thompson), London, 1950, pp. 290 f.

It should be pointed out that the primary motive behind the Federal approach was the desire to ground the doctrine of original sin upon a wider basis than that of a mere natural union with Adam. For this reason the covenant theologians spoke of a representative union of a judicial nature, whereby Adam was the representative of all men; so that there sinned with him all whom he represented, on the basis of the principle enunciated by J.H. Heidegger: "One who is represented as doing or being acted upon may also be regarded as himself doing or being acted upon. To represent is with a certain force of law to exhibit the presence of that which is not present."[15]

At the same time the covenant theologians were careful to maintain that Adam's first sin was not imputed to his posterity on the basis of representative union alone, since such presupposes the natural, or seminal, union — it being unjust for the sin of either man or angel to be deemed another's were there no natural relationship. The covenant is not the result of an arbitrary construction super-imposed upon nature, but inherent in nature. There was thus a strong Augustinian element in the Federal position, which nevertheless went beyond Augustine.[16]

The distinctive Federal doctrine of original sin is not clearly enunciated in the Westminster Confession of Faith,[17] but it is explicitly set forth in the Larger Catechism, where one can clearly see Augustinian and Federal elements closely intertwined. We read, "The covenant being

---

15. *Ibid.*, p. 313.

16. For example, see the position of John Owen, *Works* (ed. Wm. H. Goold), Vol. 10, New York, 1852, pp. 68-82; Chapter VII of *A Display of Arminianism* (1642); and Vol. 5 on *Justification* (1677), pp. 166-171, 323-325, *et al.* It should be noted that there does seem to be some shift between these two works, from an Augustinian to a more Federal emphasis.

17. The covenant of works is mentioned in the Confession, but its relationship to the doctrine of original sin is not clearly set forth (VII, i, ii; XIX, i). The Confession simply traces original sin back to the special sin of our first parents, with no mention of the covenant of works: "They being the root of all mankind, the guilt of this sin was imputed; and the same death in sin, and corrupted nature, conveyed to all their posterity descending from them by ordinary generation" (VI, iii). Unless otherwise noted, all references to the Westminster Standards follow the text and punctuation of *The Confession of Faith*, etc., The Publications Committee of the Free Presbyterian Church of Scotland, 1967. Where the Latin text is referred to, it follows H. A. Niemeyer (ed.), *Collectio Confessionum in Ecclesiis Reformatis Publicatarum, Lipsiae*, 1840, Appendix.

made with Adam, as a publick person, not for himself only, but for his posterity, all mankind descending from him by ordinary generation, sinned in him, and fell with him in that first transgression" (Q. 22). The fallen state of men is described as follows:

> The sinfulness of that estate whereinto man fell, consisteth in the guilt of Adam's first sin (*consistit in reatu primi peccati, quod admisit Adamus*), the want of that righteousness wherein he was created, and the corruption of his nature, whereby he is utterly indisposed, disabled, and made opposite unto all that is spiritually good, and wholly inclined to all evil, and that continually; which is commonly called *Original Sin*, and from which do proceed all actual transgressions (Q. 25).

About the time that the Westminster Standards were published there arose in the Reformed Churches of France a controversy over the nature of the imputation of Adam's sin, that is over the precise relationship between the guilt of Adam's first sin and the corruption of nature belonging to his posterity. The occasion of this controversy was Josua Placaeus' distinction between *immediate*, or antecedent, and *mediate*, or consequent, imputation.[18] Placaeus himself held to the latter, that is, the doctrine that Adam's sin is imputed to his posterity through the medium of that hereditary corruption inherited from him. There is a mediate imputation of the sin of Adam accruing to each man by virtue of his own innate corruption which is the remote result of Adam's first actual sin by way of his transmitted corruption. In other words, the guilt of Adam's first sin and our own individual moral corruption are in this way construed to be one. Thus the imputation of Adam's sin means nothing more

---

18. The distinction was formulated by Josua Placaeus (*De imputatione primi peccati Adami, disputatio bipartu* in *Opera Omnia*, Tom. I, Franeker, 1699, p. 173) as follows: "If by the first sin of Adam, his first actual sin be meant, and not his habitual sin which followed it, then imputation must be distinguished into *immediate* or antecedent, and *mediate* or consequent. The first imputation occurs immediately, that is without the medium of any corruption. The last imputation occurs mediately, that is through the medium of hereditary and inward corruption The former precedes inward and hereditary corruption, in the order of nature; the latter follows it. The former is the cause of inward and habitual corruption; the latter is the effect." Quoted in Shedd, *op. cit.*, p. 159. See J. Murray. *The Imputation of Adam's Sin*, Grand Rapids, 1959, pp. 43 f.

than our being held accountable for our own sin which just happens to be the result of Adam's initial transgression.

The opposition to Placaeus was especially forceful in the Swiss Reformed Church to the point of assuming confessional expression in the *Formula Consensus Helvetica* (1675), which explicitly rejects mediate imputation in favor of the antecedent and immediate imputation of Adam's sin.[19] That sin is said to be imputed to the race immediately, that is, without the medium of hereditary corruption and antecedent to it. This rejection of mediate imputation stems from the fear of endangering the doctrine of original sin by pulling its legal basis out from under it. For how can there be any true original sin, or corruption, if there is no antecedent original guilt immediately imputed to all "by the mysterious and just judgment of God"?[20] Original corruption must be the penal result of an antecedently imputed original guilt. One of the foremost expounders of this doctrine was François Turretin of Geneva, who maintains that the doctrine of Placaeus is a denial of the imputation of Adam's sin, since on his view we are not guilty of it, but only of our individual original corruption, the guilt of which is imputed to us.[21]

The specifically *Wesleyan* approach to the problem of original sin was promulgated in the eighteenth century in response to the early modern attack on the traditional doctrine led by John Taylor.[22] Wesley

---

19. Article XII reads as follows: "Accordingly we can not, without harm to Divine truth, give assent to those who deny that Adam represented his posterity by appointment of God (*ex institutione Dei*), and that his sin is imputed, therefore, *immediately* to his posterity; and under the term *imputation mediate* and *consequent* not only destroy the imputation of the first sin, but also expose the doctrine (*assertio*) of hereditary corruption to great danger." J. H. Leith (ed.), *Creeds of the Churches*, New York, 1963, p. 314. For the Latin see Niemeyer, *op. cit.*, p. 733.

20. Art. X; cf. Leith, *op. cit.*, p. 313.

21. François Turrettino, *Institutio Theologiae Elencticae*, Amstelodami 1701, (IX, IX, vi); where the Geneva theologian continues, "For it is one thing to lie under exposure to the wrath and condemnation of God, on account of inherent and native corruptions, propagated by generation; another, on account of the sin of Adam imputed to us." We follow the unpublished English translation by G.M. Giger, produced in mimeographed form by Pittsburgh Theological Seminary (ed. J.H. Gerstner).

22. John Taylor, *The Scripture-Doctrine o f Original Sin*, London, 1741. Cf. H. S. Smith, *Changing Conceptions of Original Sin: A Study in American Theology Since 1750*, New York, 1955, "The Impact of John Taylor" (pp. 10 ff) and "The Spread of Taylorism" (pp. 37 ff). Taylor's work is simply an eighteenth century restatement of

accepted the representative headship of Adam distinctive to the Federal doctrine, but seeks to justify it with an appeal to the Arminian doctrine of universal redemption. Because Christ represented all, it is in no way unjust that Adam represented all, for it is possible for all men to regain in Christ what they lost in Adam. Though Wesley admits that he cannot really comprehend how mankind can be justly brought under the divine displeasure for Adam's sin, he believes that the simple consideration of God's universal provision of redemption totally resolves the difficulty.[23]

Finally, there is the New England approach developed by certain of the "New Divinity" followers of Jonathan Edwards, chiefly Samuel Hopkins and Nathanael Emmons; a view which, obviously, cannot be understood apart from Edwards' distinctive contributions. For while it is true that Edwards' followers went far beyond him in their doctrine of original sin, it is nevertheless clear that the main features of their distinctive approach to the problem stem from ideas put forward by him, which they developed, perhaps perverted, to form their own doctrine.

In attempting to elucidate the doctrine of the imputation of Adam's first sin, Edwards makes a distinction between initial corruption, by virtue of oneness with Adam, which corruption is the ground of original guilt; and confirmed corruption, that is, a corrupt nature, which nature is the penal result of that original guilt — which, it must be remembered, belongs to the individual on the basis of his participation in the guilt of Adam's first sin. So then, as the pattern in Adam was initial corruption resulting in guilt, in turn resulting in a corrupt nature, just so the same pattern holds for his posterity: Adam's sin, including both initial corruption and guilt, is imputed to posterity, resulting in their corruption of nature, on the ground of the union between the root and branches of the race.[24] This distinction, interestingly enough, was not taken up by the New Divinity men perhaps because they denied, in ef-

---

Pelagianism.

23. John Wesley, *Works*, Vol. IX (Original Sin), London (Wesleyan Methodist Book-Room), and, pp. 284 f.: "He has provided a Savior for them all; and this fully acquits both his justice and his mercy." Cf. pp. 315, 326, 332.

24. Jonathan Edwards, *Works*, Vol. I (10th ed.), London, 1865, pp. 220 f. (from *The Great Christian Doctrine of Original Sin Defended*, 1758). For a recent discussion of this distinction, see Murray, *op. cit.*, pp. 52 ff.

fect, that Adam's sin is in any sense imputed to his posterity.[25]

But they did latch on to Edwards' notion of *consent*. He had spoken of "the first being of an evil disposition in a child of Adam, whereby he is disposed to approve the sin of his first father, so far as to imply a full and perfect consent of heart to it."[26] By this he meant the consent which we have all given to Adam's sin by virtue of our individual participation in it on the basis of the oneness between us. We are thus born in a state of attitude of consent. But the New Divinity construed it to mean that voluntary consent of individuals to Adam's sin when they themselves come to the age of moral agency. According to Samuel Hopkins, Adam's sin renders individual men no more guilty than they would have been if Adam had never sinned and each were the first sinner who ever existed.[27] It is obvious that this approach rests on an assumption of the so-called exercise scheme, that all sin consists in sinning. Or as Emmons expressed it, "All sin consists in the free, voluntary exercises of selfishness."[28]

With respect to the nature of the union between Adam and the race, Edwards affirms that we know from scripture that "a constituted oneness or identity" does in fact exist; and rather than remain agnostic on the how of such a oneness, he attempts to explain it by an appeal to

---

25. Nor was the distinction taken up in the American Presbyterian theology of the nineteenth century. It is only mentioned here because of its rediscovery by John Murray in the twentieth century. See below, pp. 94 f., n. 39.

26. Edwards, *op. cit.*, p. 221.

27. Samuel Hopkins, *Works*, Vol. I, Boston, 1854, p. 230: "If the sinfulness of all the posterity of Adam was certainly connected with his sinning, this does not make them sinners before they actually are sinners; and when they actually become sinners, they themselves are the sinners, it is their own sin, and they are as blameable and guilty as if Adam had never sinned, and each one were the first sinner that ever existed. The children of Adam are not answerable for his sin, and it is not their sin any further than they approve of it by sinning as he did. In this way only they become guilty of his sin, viz., by approving of what he did, and joining with him in rebellion." Cf. p. 235.

28. Nathanael Emmons, *Works*, Vol. IV, Boston, 1842, p. 502. Or as otherwise expressed: "Holiness and sin consist in free voluntary exercises." Frank H. Foster, *A Genetic History of the New England Theology*, Chicago, 1907, pp. 345 ff. It must be noted that not all so-called New Divinity men held to the exercise scheme of Hopkins and Emmons. For instance, Leonard Woods, who had a profound influence on later Presbyterian theology, held to the *taste* scheme, whereby sin consists in evil tastes inherent in the child at birth. L. Woods, *Works*, Boston, 1854; cf. Foster, *op. cit.*, pp. 357 fl.

the sovereign will and immediate agency of God, which, he maintains, is the sole cause of any oneness or identity within the sphere of created substance. Therefore, "personal identity, and so the derivation of the pollution and guilt of past sins in the same persons, depends on the arbitrary divine constitution." It is this divine constitution which renders Adam's sin, in its initial depravity and guilt, truly ours.[29]

The New Divinity, on the other hand, maintained that we are all, according to Romans 5, constituted sinners through such a divine constitution in the sense that God arranged that Adam's sin should be the certain occasion for the initial voluntary rebellion of each individual of the race, having Himself established an infallible connection between the two; so that the sin of the race consequent upon Adam's sin is actual sin, that is, sinning after the likeness of his first sinful act. According to the divine arrangement, Adam's sin infallibly guarantees that each of us will sin in imitation of him. The consent which we render to this transgression occurs at our first actual sin, and not when Adam sinned on the basis of a direct solidarity with him.

It should be mentioned that it was the New Haven version of the New England approach which especially provoked discussion among the Presbyterians. This approach is neatly summarized in Nathaniel Taylor's sermon *Concio ad Clerum* published in 1829. Its contents need not be reproduced here since they are amply represented among the Presbyterians by the radical version of the New School theology.[30]

Now the American Presbyterian Church adopted the Westminster Standards as a matter of course in the early part of the eighteenth century. Her position on the question of original sin was succinctly expressed by Jonathan Dickinson: "We are guilty, not merely as Descendants from Adam; but as being naturally, as well as legally, in him when he violated the first Covenant."[31] Her preachers, such as Gilbert Tennent, went about preaching the gospel on the basis of the fall of our

---

29. Edwards, *op cit.*, pp. 20, 223 f.

30. See below, pp. 16 ff, where there is a summary of the version propounded by Albert Barnes. Cf. N. Taylor, *Concio ad Clerum* (A Sermon Delivered in the Chapel of Yale College, Sept. 10, 1828), New Haven, 1828. For a fuller statement of Taylor's theology, see *Lectures on the Moral Government of God* (2 vols.), New York, 1859.

31. Quoted from *The True Scripture-Doctrine Concerning Important Points of Christian Faith* (Boston, 1741) by H. S. Smith, *op. cit.*, p. 6.

first parents which constituted a "perfidious BREACH OF COVE-
NANT."[32]

Accordingly, there was no significant debate among American
Presbyterians on the subject of original sin during the eighteenth century.
It was not until the nineteenth century that the Church produced theologians who wrote extensively on the problem of original sin. This nineteenth century interest was occasioned by the New England theology and
followed in its wake. From this interest there arose a prolonged debate
within the Church over the nature of our connection with Adam and the
imputation of Adam's sin. Benjamin B. Warfield, who in his day was as
familiar with American Presbyterian theology as any man alive, mentions that in the course of the debate four distinct positions arose, each
represented by "theologians of distinction":

> These are (1) the "Federalistic," characterized by its adher-
> ence to the doctrine of "immediate imputation," represented, for exam-
> ple, by Dr. Charles Hodge; (2) the "New School," characterized by its
> adherence to the doctrine of "mediate imputation," represented, for
> example, by Dr. Henry B. Smith; (3) the "Realistic," which teaches
> that all mankind were present in Adam as generic humanity, and
> sinned in him, and are therefore guilty of his and their common sin,
> represented, for example, by Dr. W. G. T. Shedd; and (4) one which
> may be called the "Agnostic," characterized by an attempt to accept
> the fact of the transmission of both guilt and depravity from Adam
> without framing a theory of the mode of their transmission or of their
> relations one to the other, represented for example, by Dr. R. W.
> Landis.[33]

It is our purpose to discuss these four positions as found in the
major writings of their chief representatives, not to give a running account of the debate as carried on in the theological journals. In conclusion, we shall add to them a fifth approach which arose in the twentieth
century. The order followed will be Warfield's, except that, for obvious
reasons, it will be necessary to discuss the New School position first. In

32. *Ibid.*, p. 7. From *Sermons on Important Subjects*, Philadelphia, 1758.

33. From an article entitled "Imputation" in the *New Schaff-Herzog Encyclopedia of
Religious Knowledge*, New York, 1909, pp. 465-467. The article is reprinted in B. B.
Warfield, *Studies in Theology*, New York, 1932, pp. 301-309. This particular state-
ment is on p. 308.

examining each representative of a position, we want to see how our specific problem is handled in the light of his doctrine of original sin as a whole. In such an analysis, we shall attempt to present some picture of the man's conception of the problem; his general mood in approaching it (for example, his conception of the importance of the doctrine of original sin); and his statement of his own position along with the scriptural, theological, and historical defense of it.

I.
The New School
Henry B. Smith

Various elements of the New Divinity and New Haven views on original sin, as well as on other cardinal Christian doctrines, began to filter into the Presbyterian Church in the first third of the nineteenth century. The result was that the Church was soon divided into an Old School party and a New School party, and by 1837 had split into two separate ecclesiastical bodies: the one adhering to the older Calvinism of the Westminster Standards, the other to the New Divinity. The New School, however, still professed to adhere to Westminster. Its position was promulgated by such men as Lyman Beecher, who attempted to state his views in such a way as to be harmonizable with those Standards.[1] But the most blatant statement of them came from the pen of Albert Barnes, whose heresy trial before the Synod of Philadelphia in 1835 precipitated the division of the Church into Old School and New School branches. It will be profitable to glance at his views, as an example of New England sentiments in the Presbyterian Church, before proceeding to discuss the later and more characteristic and conciliatory position of Henry B. Smith.

In early 1829, not long after the publication of Nathaniel Taylor's controversial sermon *Concio ad Clerum*, Albert Barnes preached a series of sermons on "The Way of Salvation," subsequently published

---

1. H. S. Smith, *op. cit.*, pp. 131-133. Edward Beecher, in his book, *Conflict of Ages* (1853), a book written in controversy with the Unitarians, attempted to resolve the problem of original sin by appealing to Origen's old theory of the pre-existence of souls. See Foster, *op. cit,*. pp. 308 f.

in book form, in which he set forth the New Haven view of original sin.[2] These views were later expressed even more pointedly in his *Notes, Explanatory and Practical, on the Epistle to the Romans* (1835). On the basis of the content of this book, Barnes was charged with a Pelagian denial of the Westminster Standards on ten counts. It is charges V, VI, and VII, all three of which are clearly sustained, which particularly concern us.

The *fifth* charge was that Barnes denied that God entered into covenant with Adam, constituting him the federal head of the race and representative of all his natural descendants. This denial was on two grounds: first, "there is not one word of it in the Bible;" and, second, "it is a mere philosophical theory." According to Barnes, "The words *representative* and *federal head* are never applied to Adam in the Bible. The reason is that the word *representative* implies an idea that could not have existed in the case — the consent of those who are represented. Besides the Bible does not teach that they acted in him, or by him; or that he acted for them. No passage has ever yet been found that stated this doctrine." All that is meant in Romans 5 is that Adam's sin is the certain occasion of their being sinners, just as the sin of the murderer or drunkard affects the moral condition of his children.[3]

The *sixth* charge is that the defendant denies that the first sin of Adam is imputed to his posterity. According to Barnes, it is a simple fact that all sin is the effect of the first sin of Adam. The apostle, however, offers no explanation of the fact, but is content to leave it unexplained. Yet the minds of over-curious men have not been satisfied with this, but have concocted the theory of imputation to account for the fact. According to them, "the sin of Adam is imputed, or set over by an arbitrary arrangement to beings otherwise innocent." But this is a mere theory. Moreover, it is not in accord with what the Book of Romans says. "The doctrine of imputation has been, that infants were personally guilty of Adam's sin; that they had 'sinned in him'; that there was a *personal identity* constituted between them and Adam (see Edwards on original

---

2. *Ibid.*, pp. 126 ff.; Foster, *op cit.*, pp. 451 ff.

3. A.J. Stanbury, *Trial of the Rev. Albert Barnes, Before the Synod of Philadelphia, in Session at York, October 1835, On a Charge of Heresy, Preferred Against Him by the Rev. George Junkin: With All the Pleadings and Debate*; New York, 1836, pp. 126.128; Barnes, *Notes*, pp. 120 f., 128.

sin); and that therefore his sin was theirs as really and truly as if committed by themselves. Yet here the apostle says that those of whom he was speaking had *not* sinned 'after the similitude of Adam's transgression.' But if the doctrine of imputation be true, it is certain that they not only had sinned after the similitude of his transgression, but had sinned the *very identical sin.* "

According to Barnes, the doctrine of imputation is mere philosophy introduced to explain the difficulties; and it is poor philosophy at that, for it does not explain, but only embarrasses the subject with the introduction of an additional difficulty. "For," he says, "to say that I am guilty of the sin of another in which I had no agency, is no explanation, but is involving one in additional difficulty still more perplexing, to ascertain how such a doctrine can possibly be just." The doctrine of imputation is "nothing but an effort to explain the *manner* of an event which the apostle Paul did not think it proper to attempt to explain." His object is simply to show that all men are in fact actual sinners in consequence of Adam's sin.[4]

As might be expected, the *seventh* charge is that Barnes denies that men are guilty, that is, liable to punishment, on account of Adam's sin. In maintaining his position, Barnes appeals to the parallel between Adam and Christ. He says, "There is no reason to believe that they are condemned to eternal death, or held to be guilty of his sin, without participation of their own, or without personal sin, any more than there is that they are approved by the work of Christ, or held to be personally deserving, without embracing his offer, and receiving him as a Savior." All that the word "impute" means is that men in fact become guilty sinners by a constitution of divine appointment, or simply that they are so in fact. If Paul's argument were that men were condemned for Adam's act, without any concurrence, then it would be true, according to the parallel, that all would be constituted righteous in the same way, thus leading to the doctrine of universal salvation. "But as none are constituted righteous who do not voluntarily avail themselves of the provisions of mercy, so it follows that those who are condemned, are not condemned for the sin of another without their own concurrence, nor unless they personally deserve it." Again, all Paul intends to teach is the universal fact that the conduct of one man may involve his family in its conse-

---

4. *Ibid.*, pp. 128-130; Barnes, *Notes*, pp. 10, 116-119, 121.

quences.[5]

On the whole, the New School theologians merely repeated certain of the sounds coming out of New England. Somewhat of an exception to this was Henry B. Smith, who has been called the greatest of the New School theologians.[6] Smith's theological education took place in New England under Leonard Woods at Andover and Enoch Pond at Bangor, a student of Emmons. Consequently, he was very familiar with the New England theology, even though he reacted against it in certain ways. For instance, he once wrote an analytical essay on the theology of Emmons, in which he says that no thoroughgoing Presbyterian could ever accept the distinctive tenets of such a theology.[7] Smith's own theological ideal was a system embodying a Christologized Westminster Confession, which he inculcated into his students as Professor of Systematic Theology at Union Seminary in New York from 1855 until his death in 1877. This system, including his doctrine of original sin, may be found in his lectures, first published in 1884 as a *System of Christian Theology*.[8]

According to Smith, "Original Sin means in theology just one thing: not, the first sin of Adam; not, the first sin of each man; but the general condition of all members of the race by birth, before actual transgression, into which they are brought in consequence of the fall of Adam, the head of the race."[9] This statement clearly sets Smith off from the distinctives of the later New England theology. Mankind is in a de-

---

5. *Ibid.*, pp. 131-133; Barnes, *Notes*, pp. 123, 127 f. As might also be expected, the last three charges are to the effect that, on the basis of the principles adopted in the preceding denials, Barnes denies the doctrine of justification, deleting from it its legal character and resolving it into mere pardon.

6. Foster, *op. cit.*, p. 432.

7. H. B. Smith, *Faith and Philosophy*, New York, 1877, p. 226. It should be mentioned that Smith also studied extensively in Germany.

8. We shall make reference to the 3rd edition (ed. Wm. S. Karr) New York, 1888. At this point, we may refer to the introduction of the 4th edition (New York, 1890, p. vi f.) by T.S. Hastings, in which we find the following quotations from Professor Smith: "My object is to make and harmonize a system which shall make Christ the central point of all religious truth and doctrine" (written at age 21). "What Reformed theology has got to do is to Christologize predestination and decrees, regeneration and sanctification, the doctrine of the Church, and the whole of Eschatology" (written near the end of his life).

9. *Ibid.*, p. 286.

raved condition which is truly and properly sinful. This "sinful condemned condition" has an hereditary character and is thus native. Contrary to the New England divines, there is both *native* and *active* sin. For a moral state, according to scripture and the Westminster Standards, may be sinful as well as an act. Thus men are born with a sinful nature: not that their constitutional faculties are sinful, but that the biased state of their faculties is sinful.[10]

Moreover, there is a genuine imputation of Adam's sin on the basis of his natural and federal headship, which justly calls forth the moral displeasure of God. This doctrine is definitely taught by the Westminster divines. All *mankind* fell with Adam in his first transgression. This fall with Adam is a fact not a theory, which no amount of theorizing can gainsay. The truth simply is, that every man, not individually but as a member of the race, fell with Adam.[11]

In this connection, Smith lays great stress on the generic and racial character of the fall and original sin. For it is evident from scripture that both sin and holiness have overtones which transcend the individual and the personal. "If all sin is in sinning with a personal desert of everlasting death, by parity of reasoning, all holiness must consist in a holy choice with personal merit of eternal life." But how far this is from the spirit of the Bible! For scripture plainly teaches that the moral government of God is not only for individuals, but also for the race.[12]

This thought is amplified as follows: "The Scriptures view the race of man as one, descending from Adam, having a physical and moral unity." Consequently, all men are in fact guilty before God as a result of Adam's transgression. The assertions of Romans 5:12 ff establish the fact that Adam's first sin was the "judicial ground" of bringing all men into condemnation. But this does not mean that "the sin of Adam is the judicial ground of making us sinful, or that our native depravity is the punishment of Adam's sin."[13]

So far, according to Smith, we have seen the facts of the case. The key question is how to put them together. It is basically a problem of how to relate the personal and the generic. The Union professor expres-

---

10. *Ibid.*, pp. 295, 299, 278, 324, 281 f., *et. al.*

11. *Ibid.*, pp. 273 f.

12. *Ibid.*, p. 287, *et. al.*

13. *Ibid.*, pp. 292 f.

presses the problem in these terms: "The relation of the race to the individual and of the individual to the race: the old question of the genus and
the individual, running back into the Realism and Nominalism of the
Middle Ages."[14] It is a question of the relationship between the Westminster formula: all men sinned and fell in Adam; and the New England
formula: all sin consists in sinning. As can be seen from the foregoing,
Smith leans heavily toward the side of Realism and Westminster. This
bias can also be seen in the following comment: "The greatest minds, the
best and most life-giving theology of the Christian church, the deepest
Christian experience, lead us to view men *ultimately*, not under their
individual aspects and responsibilities, but in their connection with the
whole race and the whole system of things."[15]

Various theories have been put forward to solve this fundamental problem. Smith rejects the Pelagian and Unitarian view as a naive
denial that the problem even exists. Next the hypothesis of pre-existence,
resurrected in the nineteenth century by Julius Müller and Edward
Beecher, is rejected on the ground that it not only lacks scriptural evidence, but actually flies in the face of what scriptural evidence there is.
Also rejected is the theory of Hopkins and Emmons, that of direct effi-
ciency by way of a constitution, not only on the grounds that it neglects
the vital, moral unity of the race for an abstract arbitrariness, but also
because it makes God the author of sin. Next the Union professor rejects
the theory of Nathaniel Taylor which he accuses of being one of physical
depravity.[16] There are many objections to this position, the crowning one

---

14. *Ibid.*, p. 288.

15. *Ibid.*, pp. 301, 304

16. This view is described by Smith in contrast to that of Hopkins and Emmons as
follows: "In consequence of the sin of Adam, all his descendants are born with disor-
dered susceptibilities, with a constitutional derangement, which is not sinful or guilty,
which has no character, but which is always the certain occasion of sinning. There is
no sin until sinning takes place, and this sinning is the just ground of condemnation.
The word *constitution* has a very different sense from that of the Hopkinsian theory.
This is sometimes represented as Hopkinsianism, but there is a wide difference, there
is a different psychology. Neither Hopkins nor Emmons would have admitted a nature,
however qualified, as innocent or without character. In the old Hopkinsianism, the
word *constitution* is used for a divine arrangement; in the modern, for what is human,
for the physical constitution of man. The older would not grant any soul before act, but
the latter brings in a soul under the first act, alleging that until it acts it is innocent or
neutral, etc." *Ibid.*, pp. 309 f. This representation of the difference between the two

of which is that it is purely hypothetical without any factual basis.[17]

Smith also rejects the theory of immediate imputation, which he represents in the following terms: It is the theory of the federal headship of Adam in distinction from the natural headship. On the basis of the former, all men when yet unborn were treated as if guilty in the mind of God and thus are liable to condemnation. In order that this sentence of condemnation may be carried out, God brings forth a corrupt race from Adam by means of propagation. In other words, "The natural headship is instituted in order to carry out the federal headship. And the sinful condition of every member of this race is a punishment for Adam's sin. Each individual is punished for Adam's sin by being made sinful." Or as expressed in slightly different terms, "Adam is both the federal and natural head of the human race, but the federal headship is first, prior in logic and thought." As the direct representative of all, whatever he did is immediately made over to them. "Then the natural headship is the means of carrying down the consequences of the imputation to his posterity. And so the corruption of the posterity is the consequence and not the ground of the imputation."[18]

Immediate imputation is rejected on the following grounds: First, it is not proved by Romans 5:12 ff., which asserts the *fact* that all were condemned on the ground of the offense of one, but does not say anything about the *media* of the condemnation. Second, the theory tends to present sin in an external, arbitrary, and *merely* forensic manner, so that the unity of the race as a moral, organic whole is lost sight of. Third, it must admit a condemnation which does not ignore native corruption and thus must adhere to a mediate imputation in some sense. Fourth, the theory of immediate imputation does not fulfil its claim to solve the problem relating to the divine justice by appealing to the principle of representation; for the question remains, How is it just that Adam should

---

views seems to suffer from a lack of precision and clarity. At any rate, we cannot go into the question as to whether this analysis of the matter is completely accurate.

17. *Ibid.*, pp. 308-314.

18. *Ibid.*, pp. 284 f., 304 f. Whether this representation is accurate remains to be seen. At any rate, Smith maintains that the Hodges do not maintain it in its extreme form: "In this country the most influential advocates of Immediate Imputation — the Princeton theologians — have not urged it in this form. The supralapsarian elements are disavowed by them" (p. 284). But Smith does not spell out the precise nature of its extreme as distinct from its milder forms.

be our representative? Fifth, the argument from the imputation of Christ's righteousness does not hold. For it rests on the false assumption that because grace is given gratuitously, punishment may likewise be given gratuitously. Finally — with an appeal to Augustine, Anselm, and Aquinas, and certain Lutheran and Reformed divines — it is maintained that the weight of the history of doctrine is contrary to immediate imputation. These all taught that Adam was, not merely *stood for*, the whole race.[19]

Smith's own view is the so-called theory of mediate imputation. At the outset, it should be mentioned that this view, learned in its general outlines at the feet of Leonard Woods, is not doggedly held; for, apart from Smith's lectures, there is a note in his papers which reads, "Neither Mediate nor Immediate Imputation is wholly satisfactory."[20]

Nevertheless, this is the Union professor's view, one which he thinks best accounts for all the facts of the case. As such it is not really a theory, but simply a statement of those facts. The position is stated thus: The human race is not a mere aggregate of individuals, but an organic whole of which Adam is, by divine appointment, the natural head. All men were virtually, potentially, or seminally in him. On this account, the fall brought the loss of original righteousness and a positive corruption of nature, for which all men are liable to penal evils both temporal and eternal unless grace be interposed. But before actual sin, native corruption is not worthy of eternal death, for until such a choice there is only that liability to punishment in which the imputation of Adam's sin consists, not personal demerit. "Original sin is a doctrine respecting the moral conditions of human nature as from Adam — generic: and it is not a doctrine respecting personal liabilities and desert."[21]

---

19. *Ibid.*, pp. 305-307.

20. *Ibid.*, p. 285.

21. *Ibid.*, pp. 315 f. It ought to be noted here that Smith maintains that this general doctrine does not necessarily involve classical philosophical Realism, that is, the assumption of *universalia ante rem*; nor the idea of a numerical identity of substance in all the members of the race. "The assertion that the human race is a *reality* as truly as the human individual is, is not 'realism' in the sense of this objection." Smith's own position is a moderate realism, holding to *universalia in re*. "*Universalia in re* is consistent with the position, that 'in Adam the person corrupted the nature, in us the nature corrupts the person.' There *was* a nature to be corrupted by an act: there *is* a nature which furnishes the corrupt ground of the person who becomes corrupt."

Thus while the sinful nature is the ground of punishment, it is not itself, apart from actual sin, the ground of final punishment.[22] Finally, in what precisely does the guilt of Adam's sin consist? "The guilt of Adam's sin is — this exposure, this liability on account of such native corruption — of our having the same nature, in the same moral bias."[23]

This view is set over against immediate imputation in that it does not take the Confessional enumeration of the guilt of Adam's first sin, the loss of original righteousness, and the corruption of man's nature, in a successive, but rather in a co-ordinate sense. Native corruption is not a penal consequence of the guilt of Adam's sin. For, says Smith, "all his descendants are born in a sinful condition, not as a punishment, but in the way of a natural connection, and the punishment of each is on the ground of the sinful condition of each, including as final punishment his own personal acts and ill desert." At the same time, it appears that in the Confession (VI, iii), the natural relationship to Adam is put first as the ground of the imputation of Adam's sin. "This is the view taken in Mediate Imputation, i.e., that the natural headship comes first, and that the federal headship is grounded upon it. It is not said that the want of original righteousness, and the death in sin, and the corrupted nature, were a part of the imputation." For the imputation, strictly speaking, is not of the *sin*, but of the *guilt* of sin.[24]

In connection with his defense of this doctrine, Smith simply says, "God's justice has to do both with our generic condition and our individual acts; but his justice is inscrutable."[25] But although his method of defense is, ultimately, to resolve the problem into the inscrutability of the divine permission of sin, he does appeal in other directions, particularly to the parallel between Adam and Christ. Just as in the fall

---

Ibid., p. 325.

22. *Ibid.*, p. 285.

23. *Ibid.*, p. 317. At this point Smith calls on Edwards for support, but he confuses what the latter meant by *initial* corruption with *confirmed* corruption of nature, or hereditary depravity.

24. *Ibid.*, pp. 283-285. This last statement can be understood to favor both mediate and immediate imputation depending upon how one interprets it. See below for Charles Hodge's appeal to the same formal distinction in favor of his doctrine of immediate imputation.

25. *Ibid.*, p. 304.

of Adam there is the sin of the race, so in the atonement of Christ there is redemption provided for the whole human race. Just as there is a common sin, so there is a common redemption. But neither is the case apart from the responsibility, choice, and action of the individual. Just as there is the sin of all in Adam, so there is grace for all in Christ; but each must be personally appropriated to have any decisive effect on the individual. According to Smith, those who hold particular redemption and limited atonement must, to be consistent, also hold that all sin consists in sinning.[26]

Thus we see that Smith's defense takes on a Wesleyan flavor: "It is not improbable that it is better for each one to be born in a state where there is a common sinfulness and in which there is a common redemption provided, than it would be for all the members of the race to stand or fall, each by himself, without such a provision." All to whom the gospel is offered will be condemned for rejecting it; and as for infants and the heathen, we may hope that they are all of the elect, saved under the provision of a common redemption.[27]

---

26. *Ibid.*, pp. 286-291; cf. p. 318 ff. It is not clear as to exactly what Smith means by this assertion. Apparently, he is assuming that there must be an exact parallel between the redemption and sin of the race; so that if there were no *state* of universal redemption, there could be no *state* of universal sinfulness, but only individual acts of sin.

27. *Ibid.*, pp. 320-323.

II.
The Princeton School
Alexander and Hodge

There were many within the Old School who took up their pens in defense of what they considered the old doctrines in the face of the New School attack. They wrote both against their New School opponents and the New Haven School.[1] But by far the most significant contribution to this cause came from the faculty of Princeton Theological Seminary, especially from the pen of Charles Hodge and his son A. A. Hodge. In presenting the position of the Princeton School, we shall concentrate on the elder Hodge in that his son did little more than repeat his father's position. But before we do so, we must introduce the mood of the Princeton School with a short analysis of the position of its founder, Archibald Alexander, whose influence upon his pupil Charles Hodge was momentous.[1]

1. Archibald Alexander

Alexander's doctrine of original sin may be found in two articles which he wrote for the *Princeton Review* in 1830.[2] In the first, entitled the "Early History of Pelagianism," he illustrates the basic mood of the Princeton School:

---

1. See H.S. Smith, *op. cit.*, pp. 100 ff., 125 ff.

2. The full name of the younger Hodge was, as might be expected, Archibald Alexander Hodge.

3. They are reprinted in P. Fairbaim (ed.), *Princeton Theological Essays*, Edinburgh, 1856, pp. 79 ff. That Alexander is the author of these anonymous articles is clear from the index volume of *The Biblical Repertory and Princeton Review* (1825-1868).

It is now, by many who would be esteemed orthodox, and Calvinistic too, considered so absurd to hold the doctrine of the imputation of Adam's sin to his posterity, that they will not even condescend to argue the point and demonstrate its falsehood. If those be correct in their views of the subject, it must create some surprise that all theologians, from the days of Augustine, who were not acknowledged heretics, believed firmly in this doctrine, and considered it as fundamental in the Christian system. Is it certainly the fact that the modern impugners of the ancient doctrine of the church understand the Scriptures better than all who have gone before them? Or is it undoubted that they are endowed with a perspicacity so much superior to that of Augustine, Calvin, Owen, and Edwards, that what these thought after profound consideration might be defended as reasonable, is so absurd as not to merit a refutation? Now we confess ourselves to be of the number of those who believe, whatever reproach it may bring upon us from a certain quarter, that if the doctrine of imputation be given up the whole doctrine of original sin must be abandoned. And if this doctrine be relinquished, then the whole doctrine of redemption must fall, and what may then be left of Christianity they may contend for that will, but for ourselves, we shall be of the opinion that what remains will not be worth a serious struggle.[3]

The cardinal point of the Pelagian system was the denial of this very doctrine of original sin. Now no one would deny that this doctrine is fraught with many difficulties which no mortal can explain. But the important question concerning the doctrine is, Is it taught in the Bible? Alexander is convinced that it is. The scriptural doctrine is none other than "the old doctrine of the ancient church, which traces all sins and evils in the world to the IMPUTATION of the first sin of Adam." No other theory of original sin is capable of withstanding the test of impartial investigation.[4]

Alexander is firmly convinced that there is nothing new in the modern denial of original sin. His opinion is expressed in his article specifically entitled "Original Sin": "None of the objections now made to the doctrine are new. The whole ground of controversy now occupied by the various discordant opinions has been gone over before." Those who adhere to the modern view will undoubtedly move further and fur-

---

4. *Ibid.*, p. 84.

5. *Ibid.*, p. 97.

ther from orthodoxy. Never in the history of the church have the opposers of sound doctrine been content to stop at their first denial of the truth. "On this account it is incumbent on the friends of truth to oppose error in its commencement, and to endeavor to point out the consequences likely to result from its adoption."[5]

In these articles Alexander did not himself construct the distinctive doctrine of the Princeton School. The formulation of the distinctive content of the doctrine was to be left to Charles Hodge. His main significance is that he set the general tone and specific boundaries for Hodge's work and inspired him to a most vigorous historical and exegetical investigation of the doctrine of the imputation of Adam's sin.

2. Charles Hodge

Hodge's doctrine of imputation can be found principally in two articles on the subject in the *Princeton Review*, for 1830 and 1831; his *Commentary on the Epistle to the Romans,* first published in 1835 and revised in 1864; and his *Systematic Theology,* which appeared in three volumes between 1871 and 1873.[6] In our exposition of his position, it would be wise to begin with the early articles before referring to the more systematic treatment in the later works.

The articles on imputation appear in the context of the New England rejection, nominally at least, of the doctrine. This denial is clearly seen in the *Spectator,* the literary voice of the New Haven theologians. It is Hodge's conviction that this rejection results from a misunderstanding of the doctrine, and the purpose of these articles is to correct the misapprehension. This mood and motive is seen in the comment at the outset of the first article: "We have long been convinced that the leading objections to this doctrine arose from an entire, and to us, unaccountable misapprehension of its nature as held among Calvinists. We therefore thought it proper, and adapted to remove prejudices, to state the common views on this subject, that our brethren might see that they

---

6. *Ibid.,* pp. 112 f.

7. The articles are reprinted in *Princeton Theological Essays,* pp. 114 ff. That Hodge is their author is clear from the index of the *Princeton Review.* We shall cite the *Commentary on the Epistle to the Romans* (rev. ed., 1886), Grand Rapids, 1960; and the *Systematic Theology,* Vols. I-III, Grand Rapids, n.d.

did not involve the absurdities which they imagined."[7]

Thus we can see that Hodge's aim is an accurate statement of the historic Reformed doctrine of the nature of imputation. To him it is simply a matter of there being a presumptive argument in favor of a doctrine's being scriptural, and thus true, if it reflects the "uniform opinions of the people of God."[8] What then is the common view?

According to Hodge, the doctrine may be simply stated as follows: "In imputation, there is, first, an ascription of something to those concerned; and, secondly, a determination to deal with them accordingly." As John Owen says, the thing ascribed may be either antecedently ours, or not ours. While in the former case the ground of the imputation is clear, it is no less true that there must also be an adequate ground for imputation in the latter, for example, the case of Adam's sin: "The ground of the imputation of Adam's sin to his posterity, is the union between them, which is twofold; a natural union, as between a father and his children, and the union of representation, which is the main idea we have insisted upon."[9] So then the union is both natural and federal, but the federal union is the main ground. The natural union is of secondary importance, "so that when representation ceases imputation ceases, although the natural bond continues." This means that Adam's sin would not have been imputed to the race had he not been constituted their federal representative.[10]

Of great moment is the fact that there are certain assertions which the doctrine of imputation on the ground of federal union does not involve. "We deny, first," says Hodge, "that this doctrine involves any mysterious union with Adam, any confusion of identity with his, so that his act was personally and properly our act; and secondly, that the moral turpitude of that sin was transferred from him to us; we deny the possibility of any such transfer."[11] The doctrine involves neither the idea of personal identification nor that of the transfer of moral character.

In the *first* place: "A union of representation is not a union of

---

8. *Princeton Essays*, p. 114.

9. *Ibid.*, p. 115.

10. *Ibid.*, pp. 121 f.

11. *Ibid.*, p. 162; cf. Landis, *op. cit.*, pp. 29 f.; and Hodge, *Theology*, Vol. II, pp. 196 f.

12. *Princeton Essays*, p. 121.

identity. If Adam and his race were one and the same, he was not their representative, for a thing cannot represent itself. The two ideas are inconsistent. Where the one is asserted, the other is denied. They therefore who affirm that we sinned in Adam as a representative, do thereby deny that we sinned in him personally."[12]

In the *second* place, imputation does not make the thing imputed to us inherently and subjectively ours. The imputation of Adam's sin and inherent depravity must not be confused. We bear the sin of Adam in the same sense in which Christ bore our sins. And who would say that our moral character was transferred to Him, or that He needed to repent of our sin? Likewise, in the same sense we bear Christ's righteousness. Thus we can no more repent of Adam's sin, as personally guilty of it, than we can boast of Christ's righteousness.[13]

What then is the precise object of imputation? Hodge's answer is clear-cut: "To impute sin, in Scriptural and theological language, is to impute the *guilt* of sin. And by guilt is meant not criminality or moral ill-desert, or demerit, much less moral pollution, but the judicial obligation to satisfy justice."[14] In the terminology of classical Reformed theology, imputation has to do, not with *reatus culpæ*, liability to blame, but rather with *reatus pœnæ*, liability to punishment. According to Hodge, "Imputation does not imply a participation of the criminality of the sin imputed."[15]

But while moral pollution is in no way the object of the imputation of Adam's sin, it is, along with other liabilities of birth, the penal consequence of the guilt, or liability to punishment, incurred by that imputation. Suffering, death, and depravity are penal evils resulting from our liability to punishment for Adam's first sin. If one denies this, then he denies immediate imputation and thus the common doctrine of the imputation of Adam's sin to his posterity.

In defense of this assertion, or "solution" as he calls it, Hodge writes:

> The evils which they [i.e., Adam's posterity] suffer are not

---

13. *Ibid.*, p. 122.

14. *Ibid.*, pp. 132-137.

15. Hodge, *Theology*, Vol. II, p. 194.

16. *Princeton Essays*, p. 157.

arbitrary impositions, nor simply the natural consequences of his [i.e., Adam's] apostasy, but judicial inflictions. The loss of original righteousness, and death spiritual and temporal under which they commence their existence, are the penalty of Adam's first sin. We do not say that this solution of the problem of man's sinfulness and misery, is without its difficulties; for the ways of God are past finding out. But it may be confidently asserted, first, that it is the Scriptural solution of that problem; and secondly, that it is far more satisfactory to the reason, the heart, and the conscience, than any other solution which the ingenuity of man has ever suggested. This is proved by its general acceptance in the Christian Church.[16]

But some are not satisfied with this solution. For instance, Timothy Dwight of Yale makes moral corruption purely a natural consequence of Adam's sin. Granted that it is a natural consequence, "an evil does not cease to be penal because it is a natural consequence." Furthermore, these men represent, as a matter of sovereignty, that which is really a matter of justice. God determines out of mere sovereignty to call men into existence depraved, and then condemns them for their depravity! Men are born depraved without any judicial basis of their being so afflicted. Hodge is firmly convinced that this is an untenable position which readily leads to a denial of native depravity. For the denial of imputation must necessarily lead to the denial of native sinfulness in that there is no legal basis, or rationale, to justify a man's being born in sin. The transition from Dwight, who held to the latter while denying the former, to Nathaniel Taylor and the later New Haven theologians, who deny both, is proof of this conviction.[17]

Moreover, the New Haven theologians are not convinced that the old Calvinists taught neither that Adam's act is strictly and properly our act, nor that its moral character is transferred from him to us. They produce a whole raft of citations to prove their case. Wherein, therefore, is the source of their mistaken interpretation of the evidence they adduce? It is simply this: "These gentlemen err precisely as the early opponents of the Reformers and Calvinists did, by insisting on taking in a moral sense, modes of expression which were used, and meant to be

---

17. Hodge, *Theology*, Vol. II, p. 196.
18. *Princeton Essays*, pp. 138-142.

understood, in a *judicial* or *forensic* sense."[18]

The Princeton professor is himself convinced that his doctrine of imputation is the true Reformed one, having been taught it on his mother's knees, having heard it thus explained from the pulpit all his life. When the Confession says that all mankind sinned in Adam, it is not referring to any literal oneness, but to a representative oneness; just as when the Bible says we died and rose in, or with Christ, it does not mean that we actually died and rose when He rose. If one wants to understand what the old confessions mean, he must read them in the light of the theologians of the day in which they were formulated, for example Owen and Turretin.[19]

The main reason why the New Haven theologians cannot accept the truth is that they assume that legal obligations cannot be transferred, and consequently deny that one man can, under any circumstances, suffer the penalty of the sins of another. But if this pernicious principle be adopted, how can Christ bear the penalty of our sins? About these matters Hodge is dead serious when he says, "Our object is, to show that this is no dispute about words; that the denial of the doctrine of imputation not only renders that of original sin untenable; but involves, either the rejection or serious modification of those of atonement and justification."[20]

Hodge's exegetical defense of his version of the doctrine of immediate imputation is found in his extensive commentary on Romans. It is not our purpose to reproduce the *minutiae* of his exegesis, but only

---

19. *Ibid.*, p. 147.

20. *Ibid.*, pp. 161 f. In this connection, Hodge reproduces many of the citations collected, for the purpose of controverting Placaeus, by the prominent seventeenth century theologian Andrea Rivet (*Ibid.*, pp. 168 ff. The title of Rivet's work was *Decretum Synodi Nationalis Ecclesiarum Reformatarum Galliæ initio 1645, de imputatione primi peccati omnibus Adami posteris, cum Ecclesiarum et Doctorum Protestantium consensu, ex scriptis eorum, ab Andrea Riveto collecto*) with the following comment: "The careful reader cannot but be struck by the distinctness and uniformity of their views" (p. 185). Upon a close investigation of these citations, one cannot help but question the validity of this sentiment of Hodge.

21. *Ibid.*, p. 143; cf. p. 167, *et al.* Cf. also Hodge, *Theology*, Vol. II, p. 201: "There is a logical connection, therefore, between the denial of the imputation of Adam's sin, and the denial of the scriptural doctrines of atonement and justification. The objections urged against the former bear equally against the latter doctrines. And it is a matter of history that those who reject the one reject the other also."

mention some of his conclusions. For instance,

> It is said that this doctrine is nothing but a theory, an attempt to explain what the apostle does not explain, a philosophical speculation, etc. This again is a mistake. It is neither a theory nor a philosophical speculation, but the statement of a scriptural fact in scriptural language. Paul says, For the offense of one man all men are condemned; and for the righteousness of one all are regarded and treated as righteous. This is the whole doctrine.[21]

It is the chief point of the apostle that as we are condemned on account of what Adam did, we are justified on account of what Christ did. "It is therefore an essential part of the analogy between Christ and Adam, the very truth which the apostle designs to set forth, that the sin of Adam, as distinguished from any act of ours, and from inherent corruption as derived from him, is the ground of our condemnation. If this be denied then the other great truth must be denied, and our own subjective righteousness be made the ground of our justification; which is to subvert the gospel."[22]

Does this mean that the sin of Adam is the sole ground of the eternal condemnation of the individual member of the race, in the same way that the obedience of Christ is the sole ground of the eternal justification of the elect? Not at all. For elsewhere Hodge makes clear that "we are exposed to condemnation not on account of Adam's sin *only*, but also on account of our own inherent hereditary depravity; whereas the righteousness of Christ is the sole ground of our justification, our inherent righteousness, or personal holiness, being entirely excluded." It is right at this point that the parallel between condemnation and justification breaks down.[23]

In this connection, Hodge asserts that no one will be finally condemned who has no actual sins to answer for. "We have," he affirms, "every reason to believe and hope that no human being ever actually perishes who does not personally incur the penalty of the law by his actual transgressions. This however is through the redemption of Christ. All who die in infancy are doubtless saved, but they are saved by

---

22. Hodge, *Romans*, p. 181. Here Hodge obviously has Albert Barnes in mind.

23. *Ibid.*, pp. 142, 150.

24. *Princeton Essays*, p. 151.

grace."[24] Salvation is secured by the death of Christ for all who do not actually break the law of God.[25] Hodge wants all to realize the standard teaching of the Reformed Churches:

> Those Churches do *not* teach that the first sin of Adam is the single and immediate ground of the condemnation of his posterity to eternal death, but that it is the ground of their forfeiture of the divine favor from which flows the loss of original righteousness and corruption of our whole nature, which in their turn become the proximate ground of exposure to final perdition, from which, however, as almost all Protestants believe, all are saved who have no other sins to answer for.[26]

With regard to Romans 5:12, Hodge affirms that all men sinned in Adam in a putative, or supposed, sense since this is the only possible way that men could have sinned in Adam. They could not have sinned in him actually. Even on the assumption of an extreme Realism, the act of Adam could not have been the act of all men. On that view, human nature sinned when Adam sinned, but all men as persons did not yet exist to perform a rational and personal act. According to Hodge, "To say that a man acted thousands of years before his personality began, does not rise even to the dignity of a contradiction; it has no meaning at all. It is a monstrous evil to make the Bible contradict the common sense and common consciousness of mankind." God cannot require us to believe that which we intuitively know by natural revelation to be absurd.[27] And

---

25. Hodge, *Theology*, Vol. II, p. 211.

26. See *ibid.*, Vol. I, pp. 26 ff. for Hodge's doctrine of universal infant salvation. For a criticism of it as not genuinely Reformed doctrine, see R.J. Danhof, *Charles Hodge As a Dogmatician*, Goes (Netherlands), 1929, pp. 193 ff. See also Hodge, *Romans*, p. 190, *et al.*

27. *Ibid.*, Vol. II, p. 212. This sentiment harks back to the teaching of Leonard Woods and is in general harmony with that of his students, Edward A. Park and Henry B. Smith. It should be noted that this sentiment is not in accordance with the preponderant opinion of classical Reformed tradition, which has, for the most part. remained agnostic on the matter of universal infant salvation. Cf. B.B. Warfield, "The Development of the Doctrine of Infant Salvation," in *Studies in Theology*, New York, 1932, pp. 434, 437.

28. Hodge, *Romans*, p. 151. For an expansion of this last sentiment typical of Hodge, see *Theology*, Vol. I. pp. 58 f.; Vol. II, p. 531.

natural revelation teaches that, "Guilt and sin be predicated only of a person. This if not self-evident, is, at least, a universally admitted truth. Only a person is a rational agent. It is only to persons that responsibility, guilt, or moral character can attach. Human nature apart from human persons cannot act, and therefore cannot contract guilt, or be responsible."[28]

As might be expected, Hodge is severely critical of Edwards' theory of identity, which in fact resolves itself into the doctrine that preservation is continued creation. It is purely a philosophical speculation along with the Realistic theory proper, which differs from it in that the latter makes numerical sameness of substance the essence of identity, a thought foreign to Edwards. According to the Princeton professor, Realism is a "mere hypothesis" with no support in the scriptures or the common consciousness of men. Also, it cannot be reconciled with the scriptural doctrine of the separate existence of the soul and the sinlessness of Christ. And, furthermore, it is rejected by modern philosophy as a whole.[29]

Finally, Realism is no solution to the problem of original sin. As intimated above, the doctrine proposes an impossibility: "A sin of which it is impossible that we should be conscious as our voluntary act, can no more be the ground of punishment *as our act*, than the sin of an idiot, of a madman, or of a corpse." In addition, it does not explain why we are not responsible for all of Adam's sins, rather than for his first sin alone. The answer to this question can only be found in the doctrine of our covenant relation to Adam, which is not a theory at all, but a plain statement of scriptural fact: that is, that "His sin was not our sin. Its guilt does not belong to us personally. It is imputed to us as something not our own, a *peccatum alienum*."[30]

---

29. Hodge, *Theology*, Vol. II, p. 536. This criticism is made in connection with a polemic against the doctrine that Christ's assuming human nature not necessarily involved His person in sin.

30. Hodge, *Theology*, Vol. II, pp. 216 ff.

31. *Ibid.*, pp. 222-226. A more comprehensive statement of this position is: "The main point in the analogy between Christ and Adam, as presented in the theology of the Protestant church, and as exhibited by the apostle is, that as in the case of Christ, his righteousness as something neither done by us or wrought in us, is the judicial ground of our justification, with which inward holiness is connected as an invariable consequence; so in the case of Adam, his offense as something out of ourselves, a *peccatum*

There were, however, those in the Presbyterian Church, who were not convinced of Hodge's position. Some inclined to a Realistic explanation; while others, though not inclined to Realism, were not able to stomach the doctrine of imputation on the ground of an alien sin.

---

alienum, is the judicial ground of the condemnation of our race, of which condemnation, spiritual death, or inward corruption, is the expression and the consequence. It is this principle which is fundamental to the Protestant theology, and to the evangelical system, in the form in which it is presented in the Bible, which is strenuously denied by Dr. Baird, and also by the advocates... of mediate imputation." Charles Hodge (ed.), *The Biblical Repertory and Princeton Review* (For the Year 1860), Philadelphia, 1960, p. 341.

III.
The Realistic School
Shedd, Baird, and Thornwell

The Realistic School began to gain adherents in the Presbyterian Church in the latter half of the nineteenth century, from about 1850 onwards. It was clearly a decided reaction against both the Princeton School and the typical New School doctrine of original sin. The acknowledged leader of the Realistic School was W. G. T. Shedd, whose programmatic essay on original sin appeared in 1852.[1] After presenting Shedd's doctrine, we shall discuss the distinctive brand of Realism held by Samuel J. Baird, before proceeding to justify the inclusion in this School of the eminent Southern theologian James H. Thornwell.

1. William G. T. Shedd

Shedd's position is to be found in the essay mentioned above along with his *Dogmatic Theology*, the first two volumes of which appeared in 1888, and his *Commentary on Romans* (1879). Like Henry B. Smith, Shedd was himself also a product of theological education in New England, having likewise studied under Professor Leonard Woods at Andover Seminary, in which he also taught before his long stay at Union Seminary, where in 1874 he succeeded Smith in the chair of Systematic Theology. His theology is a decided reaction against that distinctive of New England. It was ever his aim to return to the Augustinian and older Calvinistic doctrines, a result of his decided dis-

---

1. Reprinted from the *Christian Review* of January, 1852, in W. G. T. Shedd, *Theological Essays*, New York. 1877, pp. 211 ff.

dain for the so-called "progress" of modern theology.[2]

The great importance which Shedd attached to his doctrine of original sin is seen by the following comment penned only a few weeks before his death in 1894:

> The great difference between this system [i.e., the Augustinian and Older Calvinistic theology] and the several schools of Modern Calvinism, and also the Arminian theology, consists in the doctrine of a self-determined and responsible fall of mankind as a species in Adam. This makes original sin to be really and literally guilty and condemning in every individual who is propagated out of the species, instead of only nominally and fictitiously so. It also makes the origin of sin, and the consequent ruin of the race of mankind, to occur at the beginning of human history. The destiny of man was *wholly* decided in Adam, and not at all in the subsequent generations of individuals propagated from him. Individual life and individual transgression, which in modern theological systems are largely employed to explain the problem of original sin, become of no consequence. They are only the necessary effect of the real cause — the voluntary determination of the race in the primitive apostasy, of which St. Paul in the fifth chapter of Romans gives a full account.[3]

This general mood is found some forty years earlier in Shedd's original essay on the doctrine of original sin (1852). The main thrust of the essay is to promulgate a new approach to the formulation of the doctrine with special reference to the nature of the connection of the individual with Adam. Yet it is not really new in that it has its origins in Augustine, but only appears to be so against the background of the newer Calvinistic theology. The error of the more modern approach is that it has sought to investigate "the much vexed and much vexing doctrine of Original Sin" from a merely psychological standpoint as distinct from a metaphysical standpoint. "For it is the misfortune of the theology of the last hundred years... that sin has been contemplated in its phenom-

---

2. Shedd, *Dogmatic Theology*, Vol. I. Grand Rapids, n.d., pp. v ff. (Preface). Cf. Foster, *op. cit.*, pp. 448 ff.

3. *Ibid.*, Vol. III, p. iii: Preface, written in September, 1894; Shedd died on November 17. Cf. p. 260: "The prime importance of the doctrine of the original unity of Adam and his posterity appears from the fact, that it is only at this point in man's history that his self-determination in the origin of sin and responsibility for it can be found."

enal aspects, rather than in its hidden sources." This has been the case from the death of Edwards onward: theologians have been preoccupied with psychological or conscious transgression without reference to its metaphysical ground. It is this empirical method which has produced the multitude of "schools" with respect to the doctrine, whereas a metaphysical method would locate theologians on one side of the question or the other, either with Pelagius or with Augustine.

True philosophy, on the one hand, and true theology, on the other, are to be wedded together in the Augustinian and scriptural doctrine. This was indeed the case in the sixteenth and seventeenth centuries when divines passed by all the phenomena and reached back to the nature of man itself, asking the simple questions: Is it innocent or culpable? Is it worthy of punishment, whether in Adam or in the individual, or not? Reformed theology affirmed that the fallen nature of man is sin itself and not the mere occasion of sin; guilt itself, and not the mere occasion of guilt. This is the ground on which Shedd himself stands, and he hopes to improve the general position by presenting it on the basis of rational, experimental, and scriptural grounds. Only on this firm basis can there be progress in "speculative theology."[4]

The scriptural basis of Shedd's presentation is Ephesians 2:3: "We were by *nature* children of wrath." The substance of this scriptural statement is said to be simply this: "that sin is a nature, and that this nature is guilt." By the formula "sin is a nature," it is not meant that sin is a created substance, but that sin in man is a "natural disposition" — that is, the essence of human sinfulness is to be found in the form of a nature in the man, a nature volitionally disposed to sin. Sinful volitions *must* be referred to a sinful disposition. To prove this Shedd appeals to the history of doctrine, our common consciousness, and rational necessity. The normal and necessary movement of our rational intellect forces us to make the *a priori* assumption that the very nature of man himself is sinful, in order to account for our conscious, actual transgressions; it is a necessary inference demanded by the very laws of thought.[5]

But the question is, How does this nature partake of guilt? That it does so is clear from the fact that divine wrath can only come upon the really criminal and ill-deserving. This is confessed to be a most difficult

---

4. *Theological Essays*, pp. 211-219.

5. *Ibid.*, pp. 219-229.

question. But the only answer that can be given to it is that this sinful nature is in the Will, and is the product of the Will. It is not depravation of the physical constitution of man, but is "the depravation of the Will itself." It is a corruption of man's voluntary powers, his powers of self-determination. Man is at bottom a Will, and this Will is the responsible and guilty author of his sinful nature. "Indeed, this sinful nature is nothing more or less than the state of the Will." As such, it is "a nature originated in a Will, and by a Will."[6]

Now what about the relationship of this sinful nature, or original sin, to Adam? That there is a connection is plain from scripture. But the exact nature of this connection is "one of the darkest points of speculative theology." Shedd believes, however, that his discussion throws some light on the problem. If we are not conscious of a sinful nature, but only of what proceeds from it; and if that sinful nature is to be traced to the Will as its originating cause, and is thereby guilty, then it follows that there is an action of the human Will deeper than the level of consciousness. "If man is not conscious of his sinful nature, and if, nevertheless, that nature is the product of his Will — is the very state of the Will itself — it follows, that his Will can put forth an action of which he is not conscious. And if this be so, it furthermore follows, that distinct consciousness is not an indispensable condition to the origin and existence of sin and guilt in the human soul."[7]

This may sound not only mysterious but even absurd. But, on the other hand, it is a fact that sin and guilt reach deeper in the nature of man than the level of his conscious volitions. And if such is the case in our every-day experience, could it not also be the case in "that deepest and primal movement of the Will which is denominated the Fall," just as in regeneration the renovation of the Will by the Holy Spirit is below the level of consciousness? It is a simple fact that the human Will fell in Adam although our consciousness of guilt is without a distinct consciousness of the process which brought it about.[8]

This is in fact the Westminster doctrine of the Fall, that all *mankind* sinned in Adam and fell with him in his first transgression. The Westminster divines believed that all men were in some sense co-existent

---

6. *Ibid.*, pp. 229-243.

7. *Ibid.*, pp. 243 f.

8. *Ibid.*, pp. 244-250.

and co-agent in Adam, or they could not have sinned in him and fallen with him. "The mode of this co-existence and co-agency of the whole human race in the first man, they do not, it is true, attempt to set forth; their language distinctly implies that they believed there was such a co-existence and co-agency, whether it could be explained or not." They did not regard Adam simply as an individual but as a common person having a generic as well as an individual character. He was substantially the race of mankind, his whole posterity existing in him, so that when he fell, the race fell in him. Thus original sin is real sin, that is, criminality, in that the sin of the race was self-determined in Adam. "For the Will of Adam was not the Will of a single isolated individual merely: it was also, and besides this, the Will of the human species — the human Will generically." Consequently, the sinful character of the race was decided at the beginning of human history in that "one seminal human nature" which was in the person of Adam.[9]

This general approach to original sin is developed with greater thoroughness in Shedd's commentary on Romans and especially in his *Dogmatic Theology*. In the latter we find there are five ways of handling the doctrine of sin as related to Adam. The first and fifth are, respectively, the *agnostic* approach, which accepts both the reality of original sin and the connection with Adam but refuses to attempt to explain it; and the *modern Arminian*, which holds to the theory of a representative union, but denies that men are in any sense guilty of Adam's sin, and, consequently, that the liabilities of birth are penal evils. It is the middle three which are of particular concern to Shedd, and to our inquiry.[10]

The *second* approach is the theory of *natural* or *substantial union* with Adam, which Shedd himself holds. He states the position as follows:

> Adam and his posterity existed together, and sinned together, as a unity. The posterity were not vicariously represented in the first sin, because representation implies the absence of the party represented; but they sinned the first sin being seminally existent and present; and this first sin is deservedly imputed to them, because in this generic manner it was committed by them. The guilt of the first sin, both as culpability (*culpa*) and obligation to the penalty of eternal

---

9. *Ibid.*, pp. 250-253.

10. Shedd, *Theology*, Vol. II, pp. 13 ff.

death (*reatus pœnœ*), is chargeable upon Adam and his posterity upon the common principle that sin is chargeable upon the actor and author of it. The imputation of Adam's sin, upon this theory, differs from the imputation of Christ's righteousness, in being deserved, not undeserved or gratuitous.[11]

From this summary statement, we see Shedd's mature opinion concerning, one, the precise nature of our union with Adam and relationship to his sin; and, two, the precise nature of the imputation of Adam's sin, with reference to how it relates to the imputation of Christ's righteousness.

With respect to the precise nature of the union, the Union professor says that "the human nature while in Adam is both numerically and specifically one." By specific unity is meant simply the unity of a species, or "unity of origin" as some have called it, which means that all individuals are propagated from a common nature or substance. A specific unity is not necessarily a numerical unity, for in the Trinity there is a numerical unity of substance or nature without a specific unity, since a specific unity implies divisibility, and the divine essence cannot be divided. But the nature of man is in fact divided as individuals are propagated from it; so that it is no longer numerically one as it was in Adam, but still specifically one.[12] In this connection, Shedd, who in his earlier essay had been rather sympathetic, is sharply critical of Edwards' doctrine of a unity composed of individual persons aggregated together instead of a specific unity.[13]

According to Shedd, the older Calvinism along with Augustinianism taught that it is the common unindividualized nature which committed the first sin. It is in this sense that the apostle says that "all sinned":

> This sin is imputed to the unity that committed it, inheres in the unity, and is propagated out of the unity. Consequently, all the particulars regarding sin that apply to the unity or common nature apply equally and strictly to each individualized portion of it. The individual Socrates was a fractional part of the human nature that

---

11. *Ibid.*, p. 14.

12. *Ibid.*, p. 35

13. *Ibid.*, pp. 31 ff, 70, 77, 80, *et al.*

"sinned in, and fell with Adam in his first transgression." Consequently, the commission, imputation, inherence, and propagation of original sin cleave indissolubly to the individualized part of the common nature, as they did to the unindividualized whole of it.[14]

As indicated, the imputation of Adam's sin is on the basis of the natural and substantial union.[15] Shedd is convinced that this doctrine of specific unity removes those great difficulties connected with the imputation of Adam's sin which arise from the injustice of punishing someone for a sin in which he had no kind of participation, for this doctrine allows for a genuine participation. The Union professor is convinced of the truth of that which he conceives to be the position of the older Calvinism:

> Original sin *propagated* in every individual rests upon original sin *inherent* in every individual; original sin inherent in every individual rests upon original sin *imputed* to every individual; and original sin imputed to every individual rests upon original sin *committed* by all men as a common nature in Adam. On this scheme, the justice and propriety of each particular, and of the whole are apparent. The first sin is justly imputed to the common nature because it was voluntarily committed by it; is justly inherent in the common nature, because justly imputed; and is justly propagated with the common nature because justly inherent.[16]

But this scheme must be taken in its entirety for its ethical consistency to be maintained. "To impute the first sin without prior participation in it is unjust. To make it inherent without prior imputation is unjust. The derangement of the scheme by omission has occurred in the later Calvinism. The advocate of mediate imputation deranges it, by imputing original sin as inherent, but not as committed either substantially or representatively. The advocate of representative imputation deranges it, by imputing original sin as inherent, but not as committed, except in the deluding sense of nominal and putative commission."[17]

---

14. *Ibid.*, pp. 43 f.

15. Shedd, *A Critical and Doctrinal Commentary Upon the Epistle of St. Paul to the Romans*, New York, 1879, pp. 127, 140 f.

16. Shedd, *Theology*, Vol. II, pp. 30, 42 f.

17. *Ibid.*, p. 43.

This leads us to the *third* alternative which is the theory of *representative* or *forensic union* with Adam. This is the position of Charles Hodge and the later Calvinism, and is portrayed in the following terms: Representative union excludes seminal union, at least with respect to the origin of the soul. It takes the extreme ground of rejecting natural union altogether. For it is assumed that our union with Adam is exactly parallel to our union with Christ. Adam sinned representatively and vicariously for his non-existent and absent posterity. In an exactly similar manner, Christ was fully obedient as the representative and vicar of His people. Therefore, the sin of Adam is imputed to his posterity in exactly the same way as the righteousness of Christ is imputed to the believer, that is, undeservedly or gratuitously. Thus the race is not personally and inherently guilty of Adam's sin any more than the believer is personally and inherently deserving on account of Christ's righteousness; rather, the child of Adam is merely legally responsible to pay the penalty for Adam's sin.[18]

Despite Shedd's great respect for Hodge, he is obliged to differ from him.[19] For one thing, the imputation of a liability to punishment (*reatus pœnæ*) without culpability (*reatus culpæ*) involves punishment based on fictitious guilt amounting to an act of pure, arbitrary sovereignty. On this point Shedd is adamant: "To impute Adam's first sin to his posterity merely, and only, because Adam sinned as a representative in their room and place, makes the imputation an arbitrary act of sovereignty, not a righteous judicial act which carries in it an intrinsic morality and justice." Common sense alone precludes any separation between culpability and punishment.[20]

Another objection is that the parallel which Hodge maintains must exist between Adam and Christ does not in fact exist. There are various points of dissimilarity, but one which must be noted is that the union of believers with Christ is not parallel to the union of the race with Adam: "It is not natural and substantial, but moral, spiritual, and mystical; not generic and universal, but individual by election." The fact is

---

18. *Ibid.*, pp. 14 ff, *et al.*

19. See *ibid.*, pp. 37, 59 where this respect comes out. It should be remarked that at certain points Shedd misunderstands Hodge. For instance, Hodge did maintain the necessity of our natural union with Adam.

20. *Ibid.*, p. 36; cf. pp. 49 f., 52 ff.

that whereas all men without exception are one with Adam, only those who believe are one with Christ. On this very account, neither the imputation of Adam's sin nor that of Christ's righteousness is an arbitrary act in the sense that God can reckon either to the account of whomever He pleases. For instance, He could not impute Adam's sin to the fallen angels. "Nothing but a real union of nature and being can justify the imputation of Adam's sin. And, similarly, the obedience of Christ could no more be imputed to an unbelieving man, than to a lost angel, because neither of these is morally, spiritually, and mystically one with Christ."[21]

Furthermore, the argument of Hodge rests upon the fallacious assumption that because there may be vicarious penal suffering there may be also vicarious sinning; and that because there may be gratuitous justification apart from merit, there may also be gratuitous condemnation apart from demerit. But while the former is conceivable, the latter is not. For while one person may obey in the place of others in order to save them, one person may not disobey in the place of others in order to ruin them. Thus while the imputation of the sin of Adam to all men is "real and meritorious," the imputation of Christ's righteousness to the elect is "nominal and gratuitous." For whereas righteousness may be imputed to men both meritoriously and unmeritorious, sin can only be imputed meritoriously, never gratuitously. Shedd sums up his argument in the dictum, "Heaven can be bestowed upon the sinner for nothing that he has done; but hell cannot be."[22]

Finally we come to the *fourth* position, which combines the ideas of *natural* and *representative* union. Although Shedd could speak in his earlier essay of Adam's being the "head and representative" of the race,[23] he is now convinced that natural and representative union are mutually exclusive notions. While both are by themselves consistent, they cannot be put together; for the one logically excludes the other. "The two ideas of natural union and representation are incongruous, and exclude each other. The natural or substantial union of two things im-

---

21. Shedd, *Romans*, p. 141.

22. Shedd, *Theology*, Vol. I, pp. 59–61; Vol. III, p. 264. It should be noted that Hodge would have also agreed with this dictum, in that he did not believe that anyone not guilty of actual sin would go to hell. Shedd also entertained the hope of universal infant salvation (*ibid.*, Vol. II, pp. 712, 714).

23. Shedd, *Theological Essays*, p. 243.

plies the presence of both. But vicarious representation implies the absence of one of them." Thus one must choose between one scheme or the other.[24]

Nevertheless the two ideas were united in the seventeenth century in such theologians as Owen and Turretin. While Owen vacillates between the Augustinian and representative schemes, Turretin recognizes that representative union is not a sufficient solution and must fall back upon natural union. Yet, along with Heidegger, he stresses representative union to such a degree that the way is prepared for the more consistent position of Hodge. On the other hand, the older Calvinism does not depend on the notion of representative union. For instance, the Westminster Standards never say that Adam represented his posterity. It is true that some of the Reformed theologians of that earlier era use the term "represent," but they are only using it in a "loose popular sense."[25]

At the same time, Shedd maintains that to reject the idea of representation is not to reject the idea of a covenant of works, which the Confession requires one to believe. For neither union, natural or representative, was constituted by the covenant of works. In either case the union was instituted by a prior act of God, sovereign and declarative in the case of representative union and creative in the case of natural union. "Hence, the so-called 'federal union' does not mean a union constituted by the *fœdus* or covenant of works. It is rather a *status*, or *relation,* than a union proper." Adam and his posterity were not constituted a union by the covenant; for they were already constituted a union by creation, and on this ground God established a covenant with them, so that the "federal union" is a secondary union resting upon a primary union.[26]

From the beginning Shedd was well aware that "a mystery overhangs, and, perhaps, ever must overhang the nature and possibility of this oneness." But, at the same time, once one is willing to put up with this mystery, the principal difficulties which beset the doctrine of original sin disappear. Once one admits the possibility and fact of this oneness, the sin of the race is seen to be voluntary in character, and each man the partaker of a sinful nature which is at bottom self-determined. With respect to the mystery of the union, Shedd muses as follows:

---

24. Shedd, *Theology*, Vol. II p. 38.

25. *Ibid.*, pp. 47 ff; cf. p. 34 ff.; Vol. III, p. 262 ff

26. *Ibid.*, pp. 39-41.

With regard to the possibility of such a co-existence of Adam and his posterity, little can be said, although the more the mind reflects upon the subject, the less surprising does it seem. One thing is certain, that the mysteriousness of the subject has not deterred the human mind from receiving the doctrine. We see the clearest and deepest minds of the church, men of unquestioned intellectual power, and of profound insight into their own hearts, drawn, as by a spell, to this hypothesis, as the best theory by which to free the doctrine of original sin from its principal difficulties: and this fact of itself constitutes a strong ground for the belief that the truth lies in this direction.[27]

The spell of the Realistic hypothesis was subsequently to come upon other Presbyterian theologians.

2. Samuel J. Baird

One over whom the spell of Realism came was Samuel J. Baird. His position was put forth in 1860 with a large book entitled *The Elohim Revealed in the Creation and Redemption of Man*. The book is bulky, touching upon many doctrines of the Christian faith, but its main concern is the doctrine of original sin. The cardinal importance of the doctrine is recognized at the very outset in the preface where we are told that the apostasy of man is a fact lying at the basis of all saving doctrine. "The doctrine, therefore, of original sin, has ever been held, by the church of God, to be fundamental to the whole system of truth; and every attempt to pervert that doctrine, or to set it aside, has been justly regarded as heresy, fraught with the most fatal consequences to the scheme of grace and the souls of men."[28]

In this connection, it should be mentioned that Baird was a militant Old School Calvinist, strongly attached to the Westminster Standards and ever denouncing Pelagians, Hopkinsians, and Edwardians, not sparing Edwards himself. He thus holds firmly to both original sin imputed and original sin inherent. At the same time, he cannot go along with the position of Hodge and the Princeton School, for which he has great respect, but maintains that the scriptural doctrine of original sin can

---

27. Shedd, *Theological Essays*, pp. 261 f .

28. Samuel J. Baird, *The Elohim Revealed in the Creation and Redemption of Man*, Philadelphia, 1860, p. 5. At the time the book was published, Baird was the pastor of the Presbyterian Church in Woodbury, New Jersey.

only be formulated within the framework of Realism, as opposed to that of either the New England theologians or Princeton.

It should also be noted that Baird attempts to ground his doctrine on original scriptural exegesis and original thinking. Therefore, his book is not a mere rehashing of the Augustinian tradition or the approach which we find in Shedd.[29] Despite his necessary dependence on the contributions of others, his work is the product of a thoroughly original mind. For this reason, it would be wise in our treatment to concentrate on the distinctives of his teaching within the framework of the typical Realistic approach to the doctrine of original sin, and to stress certain aspects of the Realistic position which were not stressed in our analysis of Shedd.

According to Baird, the scriptures plainly teach that we were so in Adam that we share the moral responsibility for his apostasy as though we had, personally and severally, committed it ourselves. But it should not be thought that, because each one of us did not severally sin in Adam, we did not really sin in him; because if we did not sin in some real sense, we could not be held accountable for his sin. The question is, In what sense, then, did we sin in him? Baird can say that we actually sinned in Adam by means of our seminal union with him. "When Adam sinned, all his seed were in him, and so sinned in him in the same *act* with him"; so that it can be said, in the words of the old Dutch theologian Van Mastricht, "we existed, and consented and sinned in the one Adam." In other words, the common nature of all men was in the person of Adam and sinned when he personally apostatized from God. With this in mind, Baird can speak of the cause of all actual sin as "the wicked apostasy of our nature from God, in the person of Adam, an apostasy in which we are as truly criminal as Adam was, because the nature by which it was committed is as really in us as in him." This apostate nature is in us by virtue of the natural law of generation whereby like produces like.[30]

It is obvious from this brief account that Baird, like Shedd, is a

---

29. It is interesting that Shedd is not even mentioned in the book although his essay on original sin had been first published eight years prior to its appearance in 1860. Hodge, in his review, spoke of Baird's book as displaying "an overweening and unfounded confidence, a great display of half-knowledge, a lack of discrimination and power of analysis." *Princeton Review* (For 1860), p. 335 ff.

30. Baird, *op. cit.*, pp. 475, 422, 529, 502.

strong traducianist, holding that the whole man, body and soul, is produced by natural generation.[31] It is also obvious that Baird's doctrine,
like Shedd's, rests on the distinction between nature and person. He
takes the word "nature" in scripture in a very realistic sense: "The word
is not expressive of a mere abstraction, but designates an actual thing,
an objective reality. Thus the human nature consists in the whole sum of
the forces, which, original in Adam, are perpetuated and flow in generation to his seed. And our oneness of nature, does not express the fact,
merely, that we and Adam are alike; but that we are thus alike, because
the forces which are in us and make us what we are, were in him, and
are numerically the same which in him constituted his nature and gave
him his likeness."[32] According to Baird, the person is the product of this
generic nature; personal existence is an accident of the substance of
human nature. Nothing may be predicated of the person which does not
grow out of the nature. And for this very reason it cannot be claimed that
the common nature, simply because it existed in another person, is ex-
empt from its own essential guilt. Each one of us is therefore justly responsible for Adam's sin. Thus Baird can write, "If I am not justly responsible for Adam's transgression, because only my nature was efficient in it, then I may, with equal propriety, claim exemption in respect
of personal sins, since in them my person is the mere subject of the action, and my nature is the sole efficient cause."[33]

We can see that this scheme involves a corresponding distinction
between sin attaching to the nature and sin attaching to the person. This
distinction arises from two distinct forms of responsibility: that of human
nature, which is by virtue of creation placed under obligation to be in
conformity with the holy nature of God; and that of each several persons,
whereby each, in a similar manner, is under obligation to conform to the
requirements of God's holy law. In Adam, human nature was concreated
in the one person. "The apostasy of this nature was the immediate efficient cause in Adam of the act of disobedience, the plucking of the forbidden fruit. Thus there attached to him the double crime of apostasy of
his nature and of personal disobedience. The guilt thus incurred, attached, not only to Adam's person, but to the nature which, in his per-

---

31. *Ibid.*, pp. 256, 340 f.
32. *Ibid.*, p. 150.
33. *Ibid.*, p. 257.

son, caused the act of transgression. Thus, as the nature flows to all the posterity of Adam, it comes bearing the burden of that initial crime, and characterized by the depravity which was embraced therein."[34]

It is this distinction between an apostasy of nature and personal disobedience which explains how we can be responsible for Adam's first sin without being responsible for all his other sins as well as the sins of all our ancestors. For it is the apostasy of nature occurring in Adam, as distinct from the overt acts of disobedience resulting from it, which render us both guilty before God and depraved.[35]

The distinction, both crucial to Baird and curious to others, is vividly portrayed in a statement of the eleventh century abbot and bishop Odo of Tournay, which is approvingly reproduced as follows:

> Sin is spoken of in two modes — as natural and personal (*naturale et personale*). That is natural with which we are born, which we derive from Adam, in whom we all sinned. For in him was my soul — generically, and not personally (*specie non persona*); not individually, but in the common nature. For the common human nature of all human souls was, in Adam, involved in sin. And therefore every human soul is criminal, as to its nature; although not so personally. Thus the sin which we sinned in Adam, to me indeed is a sin of nature, but in him a personal sin. In Adam it is more criminal, in me less so; for in him, it was not I who now am, but that which I am (*non qui sum sed quad sum*), that sinned. There sinned in him, not I, but this which is I (*non ego, sed hoc; quad sum ego*). I sinned as (generically) man, and not as Odo (*Peccavi homo non Odo*). My substance sinned, but not my person (*Peccavi substantia non persona*); and since the substance does not exist otherwise than in a person, the sin of my substance (*peccatum substantiæ*) attaches to my person, although not a personal sin. For a personal sin is such as — not that which I am — but I who now am, commit — in which Odo, and not humanity (*Odo non homo*), sins — in which I a person, and not a nature, sin. But inasmuch as there is no person without a nature, the sin of a person is also the sin of a nature, although it is not a sin of nature (*peccatum personæ est etiam naturæ, sed non naturale*).[36]

---

34. *Ibid.*, p. 256.
35. *Ibid.*, pp. 507 ff.
36. *Ibid.*, pp. 27 f.

With respect to the nature of the Realistic union between Adam and the race, Baird believes that it is analogous to that subsisting between the Father and the Son on the one hand and Christ and His people on the other. Just as the Son is one with the Father in one undivided essence communicated in eternal generation, the elect are one with Christ through their communion in one undivided Spirit imparted in regeneration (John 17:21-23). Likewise, the race is one with Adam in a community of nature, which, though originally one in Adam, is communicated to them through natural generation. In all three cases there is a substantial and not merely a constructive union. The purpose of this remarkable resemblance is to reveal the inner nature of the Triune God, or the unfolding mystery of *Elohim Revealed.*[37]

It is pertinent at this point to inquire into the legal aspect of the union between Adam and the race. What about Adam's covenant headship? In this regard Baird appeals to the classic Reformed concept of the covenant of nature.[38] Adam was the covenant head of the race by virtue of his natural headship. The representative relationship is consented in the natural. It is false to maintain as do some orthodox theologians, that the representative character of Adam did not exist until the positive provision was made regarding the tree of knowledge. For "we are not held accountable for Adam's breach of the covenant, in consequence of the transaction respecting the tree; but because of the inscription of the covenant in Adam's nature, and our in-being in him, in whose nature it was inscribed."[39]

---

37. *Ibid.*, pp. 322 f.; cf. 428 ff. Here Baird obviously parts company with Shedd.

38. For instance, he appeals to Turretin: "The covenant of nature is that which God the Creator made with innocent man as his creature, concerning his happiness and endowment with life eternal, upon condition of a perfect personal obedience. It is called natural, not on account of a natural obligation — which God cannot owe to man — but because it was implanted in the nature of man as he was first made by God, and in his integrity or unbroken strength" (*Institutio Theologiæ Elencticæ*, VIII, III, v). *Ibid.*, p. 288. Cf. p. 305 ff, "Adam the Covenant Head of the Race." This is one of the most crucial chapters in the book. Whether Baird properly interprets the seventeenth century divines is a real question.

39. *Ibid.*, p. 311. Cf. "The point which we now propose to establish, is that we were federally in Adam by virtue of his investiture with our common nature, with the covenant inscribed in it — that the covenant being written on his nature, and provision made, in the parental relation, for the transmission to us of that nature, thus bound in covenant — the necessary effect of the whole arrangement was, to constitute Adam

Thus we must never separate Adam's federal office from his natural headship. For by virtue of his natural headship Adam stood as the representative of the race. In this connection, Baird appeals to a principle of representation recognized everywhere in scripture: namely, that "community in a propagated nature constitutes such a union, or oneness, as immediately involves the possessor in all the relations, moral and legal, of that nature, in the progenitor, whence it springs." This principle applies both to Adam and the race and to Christ and His people.[40] It means, for one thing, contrary to some, that God cannot, by the mere exercise of His pleasure, make Adam our representative if He was not natively so. It also means that Eve, since she was formed out of Adam's person and not generated from him, is to be comprehended as an integral part of his representative headship.[41]

It is to be noted that the fact that the federal headship is dependent on the natural headship does not involve the mediate imputation of Adam's sin, but rather supports immediate imputation. For the liabilities derived from Adam are in the same order in us as they were in him, namely first the guilt of apostasy and then depravity of nature. "If his nature was first guilty of apostasy and then of consequent depravity and sin, it will be so as it flows to us."[42]

Finally, Baird is adamant against Hodge's doctrine that we are not really guilty of Adam's sin, but only liable to its punishment. For it denies the proper distinction between the divine sovereignty and the divine justice. It is unquestionable that God as Sovereign can do what He wills with His own. But God as Judge cannot impute sin at His sovereign will, but only on just grounds. His judgments are ever according to truth. "If sin is by justice imputed, it is for the reason that it is really to be found there." No man can be liable to the punishment of Adam's sin in-

---

our federal head, by virtue of the parental relation thus characterized."

40. *Ibid.*, p. 317.

41. *Ibid.*, pp. 329, 322 ff. For Baird's concept of representation see pp. 327 ff. These comments are directed against Hodge who claimed, in effect, that our being represented by Adam without our consent is a mere fact of God's sovereign administration. See Hodge, *Romans*, p. 182.

42. *Ibid.*, p. 505. This argument sounds strangely like Edwards' distinction between initial and confirmed depravity, only Baird uses different terminology detrimental to his argument. At any rate, Hodge was not convinced, *Princeton Review* (For 1860), pp. 335 ff.

sofar as it was Adam's personal sin alone. "The parallel doctrine, in which the righteousness of Christ is, by free gift, made really ours, in order to justification, renders it necessary that Adam's sin should really be ours, in order to our being condemned by it."[43]

Thus we can see that neither justification nor condemnation can take place except upon the ground of the intrinsic justice of the case. As Baird puts it:

> He who supposes that God's dealings with his creatures are, in any case or manner, controlled by relations, or imagined relations, not in accordance with the intrinsic state of the case, as it is, in every respect, not only denies that the judgments of God are according to truth, but involves himself in the further conclusion that the Almighty is without a moral nature at all. For, to imagine that he can look on one as guilty, in a matter in which he is not guilty, or liable to be punished as a sinner, when in fact he is not a sinner, is to assume, that holiness is no more in harmony with God's nature than sin, truth no more pleasing to him than error.[44]

3. James H. Thornwell

Baird's *Elohim Revealed* was reviewed at great length in the *Southern Presbyterian Review* by James H. Thornwell, professor at Columbia Seminary.[45] We need not enter into all the fine points of his criticism, but only mention those comments which contribute to our comprehension of Thornwell's own understanding of the nature of our interest in Adam's sin.

Despite many good points in Baird's book, Thornwell thinks that he has failed in his presumptuous claim to clear away all the diffi-

---

43. *Ibid.*, pp. 492 f.

44. *Ibid.*, pp. 330 f. Baird also held the same outlook with respect to the imputation of sin to Christ: "Unless Christ occupied such a relation to the sins of his people that they may in some proper sense, be called his sins, they cannot be imputed to him, nor punished in him" (p. 607; cf. pp. 440, 490). It is this general principle that nothing can be legally imputed to a man which is not morally and subjectively his own that disturbs Hodge (*Princeton Review*, 1860, pp. 368 ff) .

45. The article first appeared in April, 1860. It is reprinted in J. H. Thornwell, *Collected Writings* (ed. J. B. Adger), Vol. I (Theological), Richmond, 1871, pp. 515 ff, "Nature of Our Interest in the Sin of Adam: Being a Review of Baird's Elohim Revealed."

culties from the doctrine of original sin. His position is ultimately resolved into "the buried realism of the past," an untenable philosophical
position which denies the benefits of an inductive approach to truth.[46]
Thornwell heaps ridicule on the very idea of "a sin of nature." As for
Baird's explanation of our interest in Adam's sin, two chief criticisms
emerge: one, it really makes men responsible for every sin of Adam; and,
two, it implies that Adam must have begotten penitent and believing
children.

As for Thornwell's evaluation of Baird in terms of his own
position, he maintains that the chief point of difference between them is
"not whether a man can be punished for what is not his own, but whether
there is only one way of a thing's being his own." Thornwell maintains
that there is a just moral sense in which action can belong to one without
his having actually committed it, so that it can be imputed to him without
his personally and actually being the cause of it. For instance, one can
truly be guilty of the crime of another on the ground of the principle of
representation.[47]

It is just this principle which renders us legally guilty of Adam's
sin in that he sinned vicariously in our place. His personal offense is
imputed to us, not our own as Baird contends. The latter's doctrine is
contrary to the Westminster Confession, and cannot escape the charge
of mediate imputation, which in reality is no imputation at all.[48]

Moreover, Baird confounds the twofold relationship which
Adam sustains to the race as its natural and federal head. The two must
not be made out to be identical in import. In addition, the Westminster
Standards teach that the covenant was made with Adam *after* his
creation and not concreated with him.[49] As for Thornwell's own view of
the relationship between the two, he says that the natural headship is the

---

46. To be fair to Baird, it must be said that he publicly disclaimed the doctrine of
philosophical Realism attributed to him by Thornwell (*ibid.*, p. 513). Cf. Baird's
statement on the relationship between philosophy and the scriptural revelation (*op.
cit.*, pp. 363 f.) in which he maintains that reason must bow before revelation.

47. *Ibid.*, p. 543; cf. p. 557.

48. *Ibid.*, p. 547.

49. *Ibid.*, p. 551. The Shorter Catechism (Q. 12) reads, "When God had created man
(*postquam Deus hominem condidisset*) he entered into a covenant of life with him,"
etc. Thornwell appeals to the Latin text, where *postquam* means *when* in the sense of
as soon as, after that.

ground of the federal headship: "Adam's headship is the immediate ground of our interest in his sin, and his natural headship is the ground of the representative economy. Adam stood only for his children, because his children alone sustained those relations to him by virtue of which he could justly represent them."[50]

God made Adam the natural head of the race because He designed to make him the representative of all mankind. "The natural constitution is evidently in order to the federal relation." Therefore, both are necessary in order to understand the doctrine of original sin. If Adam is considered as our parent alone, there is no explanation as to why we are guilty of his first sin rather than any other. The natural relationship cannot bear the load of hereditary sin alone. The case must involve more than the parent-child relationship: "The two relations together, the natural and the federal, explain the whole case as far as God has thought proper to reveal it. I am guilty because Adam represented me. Adam represented me because I am his child. Birth unites me to him as faith unites me to Christ. The union in each case is the basis of the covenant, and the covenant is the immediate ground of the condemnation or acceptance."[51]

Now since this criticism of Baird sounds much like Charles Hodge, the question may properly be asked, Why place Thornwell within the Realistic School? Is he not clearly an advocate of the Princeton position? The answer to this question will be seen, as we turn to Thornwell's *Theological Lectures* which were the last productions of his pen before

---

50. *Ibid.*, p. 553.

51. *Ibid.*, pp. 554 f.; cf. 271 ff. Cf. also the comment (*ibid.*, pp. 478 f.) in Thornwell's review of R. J. Breckinridge's theology: "The truth to us seems to be that the moral character of the race is determined by the federal, and not the natural, relations with Adam, and that inherent depravity is the judicial result, and not the formal ground of the imputation of his sin. Natural headship, in our judgment, does nothing more than define the extent of the federal representation It answers the question, Who are included in the covenant? Those descending from Adam by ordinary generation. But apart from the idea of trusteeship, or federal headship, Adam, it appears to us, would have been no more than any other parent. There is nothing in the single circumstance of being first in a series to change the character of the relation, and no reason, therefore, why a first father, considered exclusively as a father, should have any more effect upon his issue than a second or third," etc.

his death in 1862.[52]

But before we do so, we should note that even in his critique of Baird, Thornwell was painfully and candidly aware of difficulties in his own position. For instance, he writes as follows:

> Upon the supposition that Adam's children are not Adam, but themselves — that they are new beings called into existence by the providence of God — two questions cannot fail to arise which have always presented difficulties in speculation. The *first* is, How can that which, now and here, begins its being, begin it in a state of sin without an imputation upon the character of God? The problem is to make God the author of the man without making Him the author of his sin. The *second* question is, How can that which is inherent, which comes to us from without as a conditioning cause, and not as a self-conditioned effect, carry the imputation of crime? How, as it exists in us, independently of any agency of ours, can it be contemplated with moral disapprobation, and render us personally ill-deserving?[53]

Thornwell maintains that an answer to these questions in our present state of knowledge is impossible. There will ever remain phenomena which our explanations do not cover. Nevertheless, the solution lies in the direction of the Federal explanation. That approach does maintain, paradoxically as it may seem, that the history of the individual does not absolutely begin with his birth. The descendants of Adam were morally and legally in being before their actual existence. Therefore, the sin of Adam produced the same judicial and moral effects on them as on himself; so that God is obliged to produce men in that guilty and depraved state to which His justice has already consigned them.[54]

Thus the covenant does explain the fact that men are sinners before they are born, that they have a history, a legal history, before their actual being. But a certain question will not be silenced:

> The only question is, Was the covenant just? That depends upon the fact whether natural headship creates an union with Adam

---

52. Printed in *ibid.*, pp. 25 ff. Cf. the comment in the Editor's Preface (p. iv): "The sixteen Lectures may be reckoned his very latest literary productions."

53. *Ibid.*, p. 559 f.

54. *Ibid.*, pp. 560 f.

sufficiently intimate to ground these judicial transactions. If it does the mystery is solved. We maintain that it does, but acknowledge very frankly that we do not fully see how. We understand a part of the case and only a part. The thing that has always perplexed us most is to account for the sense of personal demerit, of guilt and shame, which unquestionably accompanies our sense of native corruption. It is not felt to be a misfortune, but a crime.[55]

It is with this same question that Thornwell wrestles in Lecture XIII of his *Theological Lectures*, which deals with "Original Sin." The main problem of original sin is that of original guilt:

> How there can be guilt antecedently to the existence of the individual — a guilt, too, which conditions and fixes the very type of that existence — is a question that must be answered, or it is impossible to vindicate original sin in any other sense than that of misfortune or calamity. If it is not grounded in the ill-deserts of the creature, but in the sovereign will and purpose of God, it loses all moral significancy, and is reduced to the aesthetic category of beauty and deformity, or the category of mere physical contrasts. The question of guilt must, therefore, meet us in the discussion of original sin.[56]

What, then, is the mode of sin's transmission? Why and how is it styled hereditary? The *first* primary question is: How is sin propagated without impugning the justice of God? To this question Thornwell has no clear-cut answer. Both traducianism and creationism have their difficulties. Therefore, "it may be safest to treat the whole matter as an insoluble mystery."[57]

The *second* basic question is: How can that which is inherited be sin? Does not guilt presuppose causation by the agent, that he is the author of the dispositions or actions for which he is held responsible? That hereditary depravity is truly and properly sin is evident both from scripture and conscience. It is "a fundamental deliverance of conscience" even though we may not know the how of it. Conscience also demands that the existence of hereditary sin be traced to a voluntary cause: "It is perfectly clear that if it must be ascribed to us, it must either be in conse-

---

55. *Ibid.*, p. 561.

56. *Ibid.*, p. 303.

57. *Ibid.*, p. 334. The two primary questions are summarized on p. 330.

quence of some voluntary act of ours or in consequence of the voluntary act of another that can be justly construed as ours. A sinful state can only spring from a sinful act. It is always the penal visitation of transgression." Therefore, the state of original sin must be penal in character, resulting either from each man's own personal transgression or the act of another so related to men that they can justly be held accountable for it — either one or the other.[58]

The first alternative which boils down to the theory of pre-existence, or an ante-mundane probation of souls, is roundly rejected on the grounds that the scriptures clearly teach the second alternative, namely, that we are constituted sinners by Adam's first transgression. We must therefore in some genuine sense be guilty of his sin. But how could that act have been ours so as to justify the imputation of guilt? What relationship can we have to him that is sufficient to ground the idea of our participating in the guilt of his transgression?[59]

First, the fact that Adam is our *natural* head is not a sufficient ground. For though offspring may suffer for the sins of their parents, they do not charge themselves with blame on that account; they have no sense of ill-desert.

Then, what about the *federal* headship, or Adam's representing us as "the type of universal humanity"? This may be the answer. "The only question is, Whether this federal relation is founded in justice." It is true that without this representative principle the race might have perished without the possibility of being redeemed. "But its benevolent tendencies are no proof of its essential justice." Can it in any way be vindicated on rational grounds? "Is there any such union *in the nature of things* betwixt Adam and his descendants so as to justify a constitution in which he and they are judicially treated as one?" Two affirmative answers have been proposed: one, that of "a generic unity"; and, two, that of an arbitrary divine constitution.[60]

The *second* answer is that of Edwards, which is rejected on ground of "the plainest intuitions of intelligence."[61]

The *first* answer is adopted by Thornwell himself. There is a fun-

---

58. *Ibid.*, pp. 340 f.

59. *Ibid.*, pp. 343 f.

60. *Ibid.*, pp. 344 f. (italics added) .

61. *Ibid.*, p. 350.

damental union between Adam and the race so that he could be justly dealt with as the representative of the race:

> He was the race and therefore could be treated as the race. What he did, it did; his act was the act of Mankind, and his fall was the fall of Man. There was no fiction of law; there was no arbitrary arrangement when he was made the representative of all who were to descend from him by ordinary generation.... Here too we see the precise relation of the federal and natural union betwixt Adam and the race. The federal presupposes the natural. The federal is the public recognition of the fact implied in the natural, and is a scheme or dispensation of religion founded upon it. If there was not a real unity between Adam and the race, the covenant of works could not, by an arbitrary constitution, treat them as one. In the notion of a *generic identity of human nature*, both ideas blend into one. Adam's sin becomes imputable, and as guilt in him becomes the parent of depravity in them.[62]

According to Thornwell, this explanation of imputation fits the testimony of conscience and scripture. Our depravity is recognized as the result of our voluntary act, it being our voluntary act in the sense in which Adam and we are one: "It makes us pronounce ourselves guilty on account of the corruption of our nature, and to the extent of our participation in the generic character of the race we are blameworthy." The only question left is "whether the notion of generic unity is an adequate basis for grounding a *personal* participation in the sin of Adam."[63]

In answer to this question, there is the answer of those New England and New School theologians who resolve the guilt of native depravity into our subsequent consent to it. But this is rejected as unscriptural. Then is mentioned the position of Hodge, though not by name. But it has serious difficulties. Simply put, it does not explain the sense of guilt which is connected with depravity of nature. On the other hand, it is recommended by its simplicity. Thornwell himself confesses the leaning of his mind to some theory which will carry back the existence of the race to the period of Adam's probation.[64]

This solemn confession is expressed in the following terms:

---

62. *Ibid.*, pp. 345 f. (italics added).

63. *Ibid.*, p. 346 (italics added).

64. *Ibid.*, pp. 348 f.

I am free to confess that I cannot escape from the doctrine, however mysterious, of a *generic unity* in man as the true basis of the representative economy in the covenant of works. The human race is not an aggregate of separate and independent atoms, but constitutes an organic whole, with a common life springing from a common ground. There is a unity in the whole species; there is a point in which all the individuals meet, and through which they are all modified and conditioned.... There is in man what we may call a *common nature*. That common nature is not a mere generalization of logic, but a *substantive reality*. It is the ground of all individual existence, and conditions the type of its development. The parental relation expresses but does not constitute it — propagates, but does not create it. In birth there is the manifestation of the individual from a nature-basis that existed before. Birth consequently does not absolutely begin but individualizes humanity. As then, descent from Adam is the exponent of a potential existence in him, as it is the revelation of a fact in relation to the nature which is individualized in a given case, it constitutes lawful and just ground for federal representation. God can deal with the natural as a covenant head, because the natural relation proceeds upon an union which justifies the moral....

But it may be asked, Do you mean that each individual will actually expressed itself in the prevarication of Adam — that each man actually ate the forbidden fruit? As individuals certainly not; as *individuals* none of us then existed. In our separate and distinct capacity his sin was no more ours than our sins are his. But as the *race*, which was then realized in him as it is now realized in all its individuals, his act was ours. How the individual is related to the genus, how the genus contains it, and how the individual is evolved from it, are questions which I am utterly unable to solve. But their mystery is no prejudice to their truth. Our moral convictions demand that we should predicate such an unity of mankind; and though a great mystery itself, it serves to clear up other mysteries which are pitch blackness without it.[65]

Thus we can see that Thornwell in the end was driven to the Realistic explanation by that mysterious pull which Shedd so dramati-

---

65. *Ibid.*, pp. 349-351 (italics added).

cally described.[66] But it must be said that his position is more in the direction of Baird than of Shedd since he fully accepts the principle of representation and other distinctives of the Princeton School such as immediate imputation. Indeed, it may be said that Thornwell's position is a bold attempt to combine elements of both the Princeton and Realistic Schools.

At the same time, there is, as has been seen, a strong agnostic element in Thornwell's approach. In this connection, he once wrote concerning the relationship between Adam and the race, "If required to specify precisely what that is which constitutes the unity, the nature and kind of relationship, we frankly confess that we are not competent to solve the problem. We do not profess to understand the whole case. We accept whatever God has thought proper to reveal, and whenever the curtain drops upon his revelation we lay our hands upon our mouth."[67]

This remark is a fitting introduction to the Agnostic School.

---

66. There are those who do not accept the interpretation given here that Thornwell succumbed to Realism. This is the position of M.H. Smith (*Studies in Southern Presbyterian Theology*, Amsterdam, 1962, pp. 152-154), who is dependent upon Thomas E. Peck, "Thornwell's Writings," *Southern Presbyterian Review*, XXIX, 3 (July, 1878), 413-448. Smith maintains that Thornwell presents "a somewhat novel view," and tries to avoid the "full realism" of Baird and Shedd. It is maintained, following Peck, that whereas Thornwell uniformly calls Baird's view a "numerical identity of nature between Adam and his posterity," he calls his own a "generic unity in men." Whether Thornwell does succumb to the essence of the Realistic position, we leave the reader to decide on the basis of the evidence presented. It is interesting that R. L. Dabney (*Discussions: Theological and Evangelical*, Vol. I, Richmond, 1890, p. 276) is convinced that such is the case: "It is after he [i.e., Thornwell] looks this doctrine [i.e., Hodge's] steadily in the face that he feels himself constrained to seek a solution of this difficulty [i.e., that of the justice of God in Hodge's view of imputation], *in substantially the same theory which a few years before he had condemned in Dr. Baird....* Here after all the stress of the difficulty on Dr. Thornwell is so great that *he adopts a theory even more realistic than the one he had refuted"* (italics added). Cf. Dabney, *Systematic and Polemic Theology*, Richmond, 1927, pp. 349 f.; where he does not state this opinion so strongly: "Dr. Thornwell, in turn, after looking the doctrine of immediate precarious imputation steadily in the face, finds himself constrained to seek palliation for its difficulty in the same direction from which he had sought to recall Dr. S. J. Baird a few years before." H. M. Smith appears to ignore the former comment in favor of this latter one.

67. Thornwell, *op. cit.*, p. 553.

IV.
The Agnostic School
Landis and Dabney

There were other Old School Presbyterians, besides those in the Realist camp, that rebelled against the teaching of Hodge and the Princeton School. For instance, Robert J. Breckinridge, professor of theology in Danville Seminary, strenuously objected to Hodge's doctrine without espousing either Realism or mediate imputation, at least in his own estimation. He maintained that while inherent sin and imputed sin must never be confounded, neither is to be explicated without reference to the other. We cannot, without error, separate what God has indissolubly united, namely, our natural and federal relationship to Adam. Moreover,

> It is infinitely certain, that God would never make a legal fiction a pretext to punish as sinners, dependent and helpless creatures who were actually innocent. The imputation of our sins to Christ, affords no pretext for such a statement; because that was done by the express consent of Christ, and was in every respect, the most stupendous proof of divine grace. Nor is the righteousness of Christ ever imputed for justification, except to the elect: nor ever received except by faith, which is the grace of the Spirit peculiar to the renewed soul. In like manner the sin of Adam is imputed to us, but never irrespective of our nature and its inherent sin. That is, we must not attempt to separate Adam's federal from his natural headship by the union of which he is the Root of the human race: since we have not a particle of reason to believe that the former would ever have existed without the latter. Nay Christ to become our federal head, had to take our nature.[1]

---

1. R.J. Breckinridge, *The Knowledge of God, Objectively Considered*, New York, 1858, pp. 498 f. As might be expected, Thornwell, before his departure from the doc-

The full development of these views, however, was not to be the province of Breckinridge, but that of his successor at Danville, Robert W. Landis, whom Breckinridge urged to write a book on the subject on the grounds of "the all-pervading influence of the doctrine of imputation, alike in scientific theology and in practical godliness."[2]

1. Robert W. Landis

Although the views of Landis were published long before in articles in both the *Danville Review* and the *Southern Presbyterian Review*,[3] they are best represented in his book on *The Doctrine of Original Sin* which was not published until 1884, one year after his death. The purpose of his work is twofold: positively, to explain the true doctrine of original sin and imputation; and, negatively, to oppose the dangerous theory of Hodge on scriptural, historical, theological, and ethical grounds. He hopes to free this great cardinal doctrine from the unnecessary odium which Hodge's speculations needlessly bring upon it.[4] In presenting the doctrine of Landis, we shall refer first to his own positive statement of his basic position, and then see it worked out in more detail in his criticism of Hodge. The central thrust of Landis' position is that of a real participation of the race in Adam's first sin, as opposed to a merely forensic interest in it. All really sinned when he sinned and on that account were constituted "veritable sinners." By participating in that event all are genuinely guilty of Adam's sin. Not that

---

trine of Hodge, accused Breckinridge of mediate imputation on the basis of this statement. Thomwell, *op. cit.*, p. 477 ff.

2. R.W. Landis, *The Doctrine of Original Sin*, Richmond, 1884, p. 5. The full title of the work is *The Doctrine of Original Sin, As Received and Taught By the Churches of the Reformation Stated and Defended and the Error of Dr. Hodge in Claiming That the Doctrine Recognizes the Gratuitous Imputation of Sin, Pointed Out and Refuted.* Landis only lasted one year as Breckinridge's successor before his health gave out. For most of his active ministry he was a pastor. Though he had no formal theological education, he possessed a huge library, with which he was very familiar, as well as an acute mind. For that reason, his book is a goldmine of historic material on the doctrine of original sin. On the other hand, the book is bulky and maddeningly repetitive.

3. *Ibid.*, p. xvi. The articles appeared in the *Danville Review* in 1861 and 1862; in the *Southern Presbyterian Review* in 1875 and 1876.

4. *Ibid.*, pp. 30, 470.

they personally existed or personally participated in it, but that they sinned in him "originally," or "potentially," or "by an ethical appropriation of the guilt of the fall." Therefore, Adam's sin is never to be thought of apart from the sinful participation of the race. It was a sin common to all and therefore imputed to all, not imputed to all and, on that account alone, common to all.[5]

But, says Landis, the *mode* of this participation in Adam's sin we do not know. We only know the fact and reality of it. It is based upon our moral, or federal, and natural connection with Adam, but the mode of that connection we cannot explain. Our connection with Adam and participation in his first sin is to be accepted as a revealed fact. "It is not necessary to maintain that the *modus* of the fact is incapable of ultimate solution. But while we concede our inability to explain it, and have no hypothesis to offer for its solution, we must emphatically affirm that our inability to explain the fact itself affords no rational grounds for its rejection."[6]

Just as in the doctrines of the Trinity and the Person of Christ, it is the fact of the union revealed and not its mode which is the subject of the scriptural pronouncement. If we believe in the unity of three distinct persons in one divine nature, and of two natures in the one Person of Christ, without being able to explain either, why should we hesitate to believe that Adam and the race have one common nature, and yet are many persons, since an equally incomprehensible principle of oneness and plurality are involved in each of these revealed doctrines?

> As it was not designed that we should either know or believe how they sinned in order to believe the fact stated that they did sin — we ought to be satisfied to leave the fact where God has placed it. The announcement of the fact itself, irrespective of all theories as to mode, constitutes an explanatory principle which furnishes the only intelligible basis on which the true explication of the doctrine of original sin is possible, as the fact of the unity and tri-personality of God, though in itself wholly inconceivable by us, forms the only basis on which it is at all possible to explicate the doctrine of redemption.[7]

---

5. *Ibid.*, pp. II, 20, *et al.*

6. *Ibid.*, p. 66, *et al.*

7. *Ibid.*, p. 64; cf. p. 35.

According to Landis, the fact itself is a sufficient explanatory principle furnishing an intelligible and all-sufficient basis for handling those great problems of explaining the calamities of the race and their harmony with the justice and goodness of God. In other words, once one accepts as a fact that the race really and actually sinned when Adam sinned, all other questions concerning the relationship between original sin and divine justice are readily answered even though one is unable to explain how the race really sinned in Adam. In this connection, one need not resort to any philosophical theories, such as Realism or Nominalism, to confuse the basic issues raised by the doctrine. The question neither demands nor admits of any solution on the basis of the principles of any recognized philosophy.[8]

The view of Landis may be summarized in his own words as follows:

> Our participation of Adam's offense is directly affirmed in the inspired announcement that all sinned, and that they were, in consequence, constituted sinners, or exhibited in their real character as such. And this is affirmed to be the reason why death, or the judgment unto condemnation passed upon all. We repeat, that we know nothing as to the mode or manner of this participation. Nor is such knowledge at all needed in order to our full confidence in the truth of the divine averment. The posterity of Adam were punished because they all alike were guilty with their parents; though in what manner the ethical appropriation of the guilt actually occurred we know not; and neither do we believe how it occurred, since the how is nowhere revealed. The fact that we all sinned in the first sin is of pure revelation; and as such we reverentially receive it.[9]

Landis is convinced that this view of the matter is that of the Calvinistic and evangelical church at large. It is the doctrine of Augustine and of Lutheran and Reformed theology. With regard to his own day, he attributes it to Breckinridge, Philip Schaff, Henry B. Smith, and Thornwell in his *Theological Lectures*, and even to Baird.[10]

---

8. *Ibid.*, pp. 13, 332 ff.

9. *Ibid.*, p. 32.

10. *Ibid.*, pp. 8, 63, *et al.*

These facts, despite the explicit disavowal of philosophical explanation, naturally give rise to the question as to whether Landis was not in some sense a Realist. He did indeed admit that he was, but drew a sharp distinction between Augustinian Realism and philosophical Realism. This distinction appears in Landis' description of the reaction of Protestant divines to the Nominalist formulation of the doctrine of original sin, in favor of an Augustian viewpoint: "They adopted not the Realistic philosophy, or rather should I say philosophical Realism, but the Realism of Augustine, whose views should never be regarded as identical with the speculations of the later schools of Realists. He was a Realist in the sense of maintaining that we really and actually sinned in Adam, and that his sin was imputed to us as participants; but not in the sense of adopting (as the later Realists did) the dicta of a mere human philosophy as sufficient to explain either the *modus* of this our sinning, or the principle of our asserted moral identity with the first and second Adam."[11]

In this connection, Landis can remark concerning the theory of Baird, "We neither have, nor ever have had, a particle of sympathy with Dr. Baird's attempts at a philosophical speculation on the subject." Yet the Church has never considered this view associated with philosophical Realism as in any way heretical. Moreover, it is "incomparably less objectionable than the scheme of Dr. Hodge, for this *is* fundamentally at variance with the word of God and the theology of the Church, as is testified *una voce* by the great body of her representative divines."[12]

On the other hand, Hodge claims that any deviation from his doctrine is deviation from a "principle which is fundamental to the Protestant theology and to the evangelical system."[13] What then is the precise point of divergence between Landis and Hodge? In Landis' words:

> Dr. Hodge teaches that the sin of Adam was made common to the race by a forensic and gratuitous imputation, while, on the contrary, the Calvinistic and Lutheran communions have, from the beginning always taught that the sin was imputed *because it was common*;

---

11. *Ibid.*, p. 344.
12. *Ibid.*, p. 347.
13. *Ibid.*, pp. 9 f. Cf. Hodge, *Princeton Review* (For 1860), pp. 344 f.

i.e., the sin alike of Adam and his posterity. This single point, presents, in fact, the nucleus of the whole question. For if the sin became common only through a forensic or gratuitous imputation of Adam's *peccatum alienum*, or merely personal guilt, then the doctrine of our participation therein is a figment.[14]

To accept this doctrine would involve fatal consequences to Christian theology. For one thing, Hodge explicitly says, "Our obligation to suffer for Adam's sin, so far as that sin is concerned, arises solely from his being our representative, and not from any participation in its moral turpitude."[15] This statement is a plain denial of the truth. The dispute between Danville and Princeton is not whether suffering is the penal consequence of the first transgression, but whether it is the punishment of Adam's merely personal sin, a *peccatum alienum* not really ours.[16]

The *scriptural* argument against Hodge is simply Romans 5:12 ff. Whereas Hodge says "all sinned" means that all were regarded and treated as sinners, the verb sin (ἁμαρτάνειν) cannot mean to become sinful, still less to be liable to punishment, but rather to sin actually. Its reference is to real, actual sinning. And it is just this which is the classic Protestant interpretation.[17]

Moreover, Landis maintains that there is no parallel instituted here between the *mode* of the communication of sin on the one hand and of righteousness on the other; or, between the *mode* by which the judgment unto condemnation is inflicted and that by which the free gift of justification is bestowed. There is no gratuitous imputation of sin in this passage. "It is not true that because God extends mercy gratuitously

---

14. Landis, *op. cit.*, p. III.

15. *Princeton Essays*, p. 149; cf. Landis, *op. cit.*, p. 23.

16. Landis, *op. cit.*, pp. 166 f.

17. *Ibid.*, p. 295; cf. the comment quoted from H. Witsius, *Economy of the Covenants*, I, viii, 31: "It is very clear to any not under the power of prejudice, when the apostle affirms that all sinned, he spake of an actual sinning, or of an actual sin — the very term sin denoting an action. It is one thing to sin, another to be sinful, if I may so speak." For this exegesis Landis also appeals to Philip Schaff's work on Romans in the Lange series. It might be noted here that Hodge could have interpreted the citation from Witsius in terms of his doctrine: for example, here Witsius is simply denying the classical Augustinian interpretation of Romans 5:12, i.e., that all became sinful, or corrupted themselves, in Adam.

to the penitent believing sinner, he therefore inflicts vengeance gratuitously upon the innocent. Paul has in no way whatever taught any such
notion." The sentence of condemnation does not resemble the sentence
of justification except insofar as God the righteous Judge has pronounced them on a righteous basis. But while we merit the former, we
in no way merit the latter. This is the doctrine of Turretin and of Owen,
who expressly says that, whereas condemnation is of nature, justification
is of grace.[18] And did not Calvin himself explicitly deny that we are condemned for an alien sin?[19]

Why then does Hodge insist that his interpretation is correct?
Simply because of his *a priori* assumption that it is impossible that the
race could have actually sinned in Adam. It were absurd to think so. But
this is precisely the Socinian and Remonstrant exegesis of the passage,
who taught that participation in Adam's sin was impossible and that
punishment thus came upon the race for Adam's personal sin alone.[20]
Hodge says that "human nature apart from human persons cannot act,
and therefore cannot contract guilt, or be responsible," and that such is
an impossible and absurd notion. But is not this just what Paul teaches,
and what the leading divines of the Church since the days of Augustine
have always taught?[21] According to Landis, Hodge is guilty of reintro-
ducing Pelagian, Socinian, Arminian, and German Rationalism. Who is
to say that we could not really sin in Adam before our own individual,
personal existence? "The doctrine itself, that we all sinned in the first
sin, is of pure revelation, and as such neither our philosophy, nor our
notions of the 'absurd' and 'impossible' can have anything to do with it.
The Holy Spirit does not teach absurdities, nor do they believe absurdities who believe what He teaches. The question, therefore, is, Has God
plainly and clearly announced that the posterity of Adam became verita-

---

18. This is likewise the doctrine of the old Reformed divine F. Gomarus: "Adam
communicates his fall and death to his posterity by nature; Christ communicates his
righteousness and life to us by grace and gift." Also A. Rivet clearly says: "There is
a comparison of the causes, and not of the mode in which the thing is communicated
to us. For the sin of Adam is communicated to us by generation, but the righteousness
of Christ by imputation." *Ibid.*, pp. 189-201.

19. See J. Calvinus, *Institutio Christianæ Religionis*, II, i, 8; also comments on Rom
5:17.

20. *Ibid.*, pp. 12, 227 ff, *et al.*

21. *Ibid.*, p. 63; cf. Hodge, *Theology*, Vol. II p. 536.

ble sinners in the fall? And has the Church received and taught this doctrine?"[22]

The *historical* argument against Hodge is twofold: positively, the Church has ever taught a doctrine contrary to his; and, negatively, it has explicitly condemned his views as contrary to the truth. Hodge's great mistake is that, first, he understands the term "imputation," when referring to Adam's sin, in a purely forensic sense, a sense in which the divines of the church never employ it in this connection. Second, he assumes that they mean by Adam's sin his personal sin alone, and not the first sin or sin of the race. According to Hodge, the first transgression is limited to Adam's merely personal sin and does not include the voluntary apostasy and crime of the race. And, third, in this very connection he assumes that the expression "the guilt of Adam's first sin" refers to Adam's personal guilt alone, and not, in addition, to the subjective guilt of the race; so that when divines speak of the priority of the guilt of that sin to the inherent depravity of the race, it is assumed that the race is born depraved as a penal consequence of Adam's sin alone. But the guilt which precedes depravity "in the order of nature," as some were inclined to say, is not that of Adam's personal sin, but of the sin of the race which fell when he fell.[23]

Consequently, if there is any logical priority of the guilt of Adam's first sin before our loss of original righteousness and consequent depravity, it is a priority, not of Adam's personal sin to our depravity, but rather of our mutual participation with Adam in his first sin, and our consequent guilt, to our depravity, which is its penal consequence — a participation which is not purely legal in character.[24]

Thus the Church doctrine of antecedent and immediate imputa-

---

22. *Ibid.*, p. 33; cf. p. 219.

23. *Ibid.*, pp. 46 f., 71, *et al.* "They held, not that his personal act was our personal act, but maintained that his sin is not to be confounded with our sin, and vice versa, or to be reckoned as in any way identical therewith, except as the guilt of the participator may be regarded as the guilt of the principal" (p. 52).

24. To bolster this assertion, Landis quotes from various Reformed divines, e.g., D. Paraeus: "And so, on account of the first fall of Adam, his whole posterity contracted guilt, and was deprived of its original dignity and righteousness, because his entire posterity sinned in Adam, seeing that they were in him. Wherefore, it was not only on account of a foreign sin, but also on account of their own (*non tantum propter alienum sed etiam propter suum peccatum*)." *Ibid.*, p. 47; cf. pp. 65, 76.

tion must never be confused with gratuitous imputation. The expression "immediate imputation" in Reformed theology before Hodge never means that sin is imputed to the race irrespective of their subjective culpability. Reformed divines never teach "a forensic imputation of the *peccatum alienum* of Adam as antecedent to and solely productive of the inherent sin or corruption of the race; but an imputation, not only of Adam's sin, but of their own sin and with him; which imputation, as they teach, is antecedent to our birth, or to what is named in church theology 'actual sin,' as distinct from the inherent or habitual."[25]

But if one rejects Hodge's view, is he not liable to the charge of mediate imputation? No, says Landis, for both gratuitous and mediate imputation are alike opposed to the true doctrine. The former teaches, on the basis of the federal relationship, that the imputation of guilt is the cause of depravity; whereas the latter teaches, on the basis of the natural relationship, that depravity is the cause of guilt, or the imputation of Adam's sin. But in reality neither is the case. Guilt on the basis of the moral, or federal, relationship and depravity on the basis of the natural relationship are to be taken together, without the priority of either, in order to explain the doctrine of original sin. Neither imputation nor sin (that is, depravity) is prior, but both must be taken together; so that immediate imputation, properly understood, is opposed to both gratuitous and mediate imputation alike.[26]

---

25. *Ibid.*, pp. 48 f. This last is a confusing statement. Does it mean that the imputation of Adam's sin is antecedent to actual sin, but not to inherent depravity; or that it is antecedent to both, in that it is antecedent to birth? The context of Landis' viewpoint would indicate the latter in that he believes that men are subjectively culpable in Adam before their birth.

26. *Ibid.*, pp. 45, 53-55. Again, this thinking is confusing. It makes no distinction, implied above, between participation in Adam's sin and hereditary depravity, and the difference between the guilt consequent upon each. Also, it seems to contradict what was said above concerning the priority of the race's guilt in Adam's first sin to hereditary depravity (*ibid.*, pp 54 f.). The above summary and preceding comments are based upon the following statement of Landis: "God finds Adam, as the federal and natural head of the race, and the race itself, alike implicated in the guilt of the first sin, and therefore imputed it alike to both — to Adam as principal, to the race as participators. The sinning was synchronous; 'all sinned,' as the apostle teaches (using the second aorist or historic tense), and thus the natural and moral headship are, as they should be, equally recognized as possessing a determining significant, which it is impossible that they should coincidently possess in either of the theories aforesaid, seeing that they resolve into the simple relation of cause and effect of both sin and im-

Hodge likewise confuses the Federal idea of representation with gratuitous imputation. It is true that the Federal view does tend to exalt the moral (that is, judicial or forensic) explanation of original sin over the natural, to which Placaeus rightly reacted, although unfortunately to the opposite error. But, in reality, with the Federal theology, "the true idea was, not that the guilt of the representation was charged upon the represented to constitute the sinners (as Dr. Hodge so preposterously imagines), but that it was charged because the guilt was common alike to them and their representatives."[27]

This leads us to Landis' charge that Hodge's doctrine is essentially the same as that of the Remonstrants and the Socinians, as well as that of the Nominalists in the Roman Church. All three teach that from birth we suffer the penal consequences of Adam's sin, not ours; that we are treated as sinners even though we really are not. Does not the Arminian Curcellaeus himself say that "the name sinner is attributed to those who are treated as sinners (*qui tanquam peccatores tractantur*), or who are implicated with them in the same calamity, even though, properly speaking, they are not sinners"?[28] Do not these heretics teach: one, that the sin of Adam is imputed to posterity *as if* they were guilty with him of his first transgression; and, two, that original sin (that is, inherent corruption) is not truly and properly sin, but only the effect and punishment of his sin? It is true that Hodge affirms that native corruption is truly and properly sin, alleging that this affirmation separates him from the Nominalists. But both alike deny that this corruption and calamity is voluntarily brought upon ourselves by our implication in Adam's sin. "But though they thus quibble," says Landis, "about calling those things sin, they affirm them to be punishments indicted on us for the *peccatum alienum* of Adam." Since there is no real

---

putation; i.e., *sin and the consequent imputation*, or *imputation and the consequent sin*, as above shown. It requires, therefore, no argument to evince that the doctrine of the Church — *antecedent and immediate imputation* (as it is expressed in our later theology) — is opposed alike to the technical theories of both gratuitous and mediate imputation."

27. *Ibid.*. p. 167; cf. 261. The doctrine of Hodge, according to Landis, is that of the Arminian Stephanus Curcellaeus in his reply to Samuel Maresius' affirmation that the first sin was a common sin: "It was not common except through that imputation about which we are disputing" (p. 359).

28. *Ibid.*, p. 243.

basis for their being anything other than penal inflictions, to call them *sin* is an empty use of words. According to Landis, it is the teaching of John Taylor and some of the New England divines all over again.[29]

In this connection, we should note that both Hodge and Landis agree that we could not personally commit Adam's first sin. But while Hodge infers from this that we could not actually be culpable for Adam's sin, but only guilty of it in the sense of being legally liable to its punishment, Landis refuses to make this inference. Thus when Hodge says that men are sinful at birth, to Landis this implies merely a legal state which has no real basis in the prior sin of the race in Adam, and thus amounts to legal penalty without real guilt, and thus real sin.

The *theological* argument against Hodge boils down to his sub-version of the doctrine of justification by faith alone. Now the Princeton professor maintains an exact parallel between the communication of Adam's sin to the race and the communication of Christ's righteousness to the elect; so that just as all men are constituted sinners not only by imputation, but also by inherent depravity, so all the elect are constituted righteous not only by the imputation of Christ's righteousness, but also "by the consequent renewing of their nature flowing from their reconcili-ation to God."[30] Just as inherent depravity is an inseparable consequence of the imputation of Adam's sin, so regeneration is the inseparable con-sequence of the imputation of Christ's righteousness. For by "renewing of their nature" here, Hodge must mean regeneration because any refer-ence to the work of progressive sanctification would not be exactly par-allel to the birth in sin consequent upon imputation, as would the new birth in righteousness.[31]

On this assumption, Hodge's theory reverses the connection between regeneration and justification and makes justifying faith either an exercise of the soul anterior to regeneration, or an exercise of the soul subsequent to justification. If the former, he denies that regeneration by the Holy Spirit is prior to saving faith, which is "a fundamental and fatal

---

29. *Ibid.*, pp. 280 f.; pp. 67, 396-398, *et at.*

30. *Ibid.*, p. 267; cf. Hodge, *Theology*, Vol. II, p. 249.

31. *Ibid.*, pp. 254, 266 f. But it appears that Landis misinterprets Hodge, who does in fact mean progressive sanctification, thus inadvertently betraying the nature of the parallel which he assumes, unless he means by "inherent depravity," not the condition in which one is born but some kind of progressive corruption. This is a clear example of careless language in theological formulation.

error" of Arminianism; if the latter, he holds to the doctrine of eternal justification, an antinomian error long since rejected by Reformed theology. In the latter connection, the charge is proved in that he is so bold as to base justification, at least partially, on an "eternal federal union."[32]

Finally, there are various *ethical* objections to Hodge's view.[33] We shall only mention one: his doctrine impugns the justice of God. Landis throws out the challenge:

> Let the serious-minded reader propound to himself, and frankly answer according to the spontaneous convictions of his moral nature and the impressions derived from the teachings of the divine word, the question, whether it can conceivably consist with the moral perfections of God, as revealed in His word and works, that He, on any ground whatever and by a mere act of the will, should constitute an innocent dependent creature depraved, apostate, and criminal, and then treat him or proceed against him as such?[34]

Such a representation of the case cannot be squared with "the moral and rational nature with which man is endowed."[35] It is the argument of Augustine against the Pelagians and the old Reformed divines against their opponents: Where there is punishment (*pœna*). there must be guilt (*culpa*); *reatus pœnæ* can never be separated from *reatus culpæ*, or, in Landis' own formulation, "the actual ill-desert of the creature invariably precedes the penal exactions of divine justice."[36] Otherwise, the whole foundation of ethics is subverted. It should be noted in this connection, that when Landis refers to subjective guilt or inherent ill-desert, he is not necessarily referring to the guilt of native depravity, but most probably to the guilt inherent in participation in Adam's first sin; whereas by subjective or inherent guilt, Hodge is referring to personal depravity of nature.

In summary, both Hodge and Landis believed that each other's doctrines would logically lead to an essential modification of the whole

---

32. *Ibid.*, pp. 254-256. 265 f. Cf. Hodge in *Princeton Review* (For 1860), pp. 766 f.

33. *Ibid.*, pp. 407 ff.

34. *Ibid.*, p. 50.

35. *Ibid.*, p. 425; cf. pp. 423 ff.

36. *Ibid.*, pp. 89 ff.

doctrinal system of the Church.[37] Landis actually believed that the Church owed to God, to herself, and to the souls of perishing men to make a "prompt and decided deliverance" with respect to the controversy lest this doctrine eat away at her very foundation.[38]

It has been necessary to deal with Landis at such length, first, because of the fascinating interplay of so many of the approaches previously discussed in his treatment of the problem; and, secondly, because of the influence of his own opinion on others, for example, R. L. Dabney.[39]

2. Robert L. Dabney

Landis' book on *Original Sin* was reviewed in the *Southern Presbyterian Review* by R. L. Dabney.[40] The reviewer manifests substantial sympathy with Landis' criticisms of Hodge's "extreme view," although he is not as convinced as Landis of the seriousness of the issue. For instance, he calls the matter under debate an "open issue," and simply says that "Dr. Hodge has obviously been incautious."[41] It is interesting that Dabney agrees with Landis' charge that Hodge's insistence on an exact parallel between the two imputations respecting Adam's sin and

---

37. *Ibid.*, pp. 77, 259.

38. *Ibid.*, pp. 469-471. The practical urgency of the situation was evidenced by the refusal of one presbytery to admit Dr. Baird to membership, on the ground of heretical notions evidenced by his disagreement with Hodge.

39. Cf. Shedd, *Theology*, Vol. II, pp. 44 f.; where Shedd lauds Landis' historical demonstration of the necessity of a real and actual participation in the first sin as integral to the older Calvinism, but laments his rejection of philosophical Realism: "In so doing, he departs from both Augustine and the older Calvinists, as much as the advocates of the representative theory. For it is clear that there can be no participation in the first sin, unless the posterity are in existence to participate in it. And the only way in which they could exist and act in Adam, is as a single specific nature. They could not exist in Adam as an aggregate of millions of individuals." That Dabney was influenced by Landis is clear from the fact that Landis' opinions were in print in the *Danville Review* in 1861 and 1862, some ten years before Dabney wrote on the subject espousing many of Landis' criticisms of Hodge. He certainly must have known of them long before he reviewed Landis' book in 1884. But, as we shall see, Dabney was no slavish follower of Landis.

40. The article was published in the 1884 volume. It is reproduced in R. L. Dabney, *Discussions: Theological and Evangelical*, Vol. I, Richmond, 1890, pp. 143 fF.

41. *Ibid.*, pp. 143, 163.

Christ's righteousness involves him in an incautious denial of justification by faith. For such an insistence leads to a conclusion which opposes Hodge, namely, that "in each case the subjective change is in order to the forensic."[42]

At this point we may mention two points at which Dabney is at variance with Landis' presentation. First, while Hodge is criticized for *a priori* assumptions that certain things cannot be taught in scripture because they conflict with man's rational intuitions, Landis himself assumes that the Bible cannot teach gratuitous imputation on the ground of its conflicting with man's moral and rational constitution. Dabney himself holds that the teaching of scripture cannot contradict right reason; otherwise, we should not be Protestant. But he defines "right reason" in terms of the laws of thought which bar self-contradictions.[43]

Secondly, Dabney does not believe that the historical evidence entirely disfavors Hodge's construction. His view of gratuitous imputation has some foundation among the later Calvinistic theology of the seventeenth century, for instance Turretin. According to the Southern theologian, "The true verdict of the history of this opinion seems to us this: that a few of the more acute and forward of the Calvinistic divines were tempted, by their love of system and symmetry of statement and overconfidence in their own logic, to excogitate the ill-stated distinction of the antecedent and gratuitous imputation. Their error here was exactly like that of the supralapsarians, who thought they could throw light and symmetry on the doctrine of the decree by assigning what they thought was the logical order of sequence to its parts. But they became 'wise above that which is written.'" For this reason, they misrepresented the moral attributes of God and provoked a number of unnecessary objections. But, fortunately, the preponderance of opinion held that original corruption and the imputation of sin were co-extensive and inseparable, rejecting the notion that a just God would gratuitously impute the guilt of an alien sin to an agent personally innocent. Most refused to distinguish between immediate and mediate imputation.[44]

These sentiments, among others which we have seen in Landis,

---

42. *Ibid.*, p. 153. For a fuller discussion of Dabney's treatment of this criticism, see below.

43. *Ibid.*, p. 163; cf. p. 277 ff.

44. *Ibid.*, pp. 165 f.; cf. pp. 255-258.

are expressed in Dabney's earlier extended review of Hodge's theology (1873), and his *Systematic and Polemic Theology* (1871).[45] Although the two treatments are fairly parallel in the content of their treatment of the problem of original sin, we shall follow in our exposition the basic structure of the systematic treatment, filling in details from the review of Hodge's position.

According to Dabney, the facts of revelation, both in scripture and history, imply that there is, under the aegis of divine providence, a moral and legal connection between the condition of the race and Adam's sin: "God was pleased, for wise, gracious, and righteous reasons, to connect the destiny of Adam's posterity with his probationary acts, so making him their representative, that whatever moral, and whatever legal condition he procured for himself by his conduct under probation; in that same moral and that same legal condition his posterity should begin to exist."[46]

The problem of original sin is thus related to this twofold condition, that is, to the two elements of original sin: the moral condition which is original corruption or native depravity; and the legal condition which is original guilt or the imputation of Adam's sin. The problem in Dabney's own words is expressed in the following manner:

> The doctrine of original sin is acknowledged by all divines to be difficult, mysterious and awful. It is liable to cavils which are hard to explode, at least with such a full solution as will satisfy the unrenewed mind. The objections to the righteousness of such a dispensation, as we suppose, may virtually be resolved into two: one aimed against the justice of God's providentially placing us in our subjective condition; the other against the justice of his imputing to us Adam's guilt.[47]

With respect to the general question as to how this moral and legal connection is transmitted to posterity, Dabney confesses ignorance.

---

45. The former is reprinted from the *Southern Presbyterian Review* for 1873 in *ibid.*, pp. 229 ff. The edition of the latter used in this study is R.L. Dabney, *Syllabus and Notes of the Course of Systematic and Polemic Theology Taught in Union Theological Seminary*, Virginia (6th ed.), Richmond, 1927.

46. Dabney, *Syllabus*, p. 317.

47. Dabney, *Discussions*, p. 273.

The question boils down to that of the origin of the soul, which is pronounced, in a spirit similar to that of Thornwell and Landis, "an insoluble mystery."[48] More specifically, native depravity is communicated by the law of propagation or reproduction, on behalf of which Dabney argues, contrary to Thornwell's objections to it. Moral character can, indeed, be propagated from parents to children. Regenerate character cannot be propagated because it is a supernatural rather than a natural property. This native depravity thus propagated is never to be separated from legal guilt, or vice-versa. For this reason, infants do not die by reason of the guilt of Adam's sin alone, "for imputed guilt and actual depravity are never found separated in the natural man."[49]

This leads to Dabney's view of imputation and original guilt. He defines the nature of imputation itself, as does Hodge, by stating that it is not Adam's *sin* which is imputed to us, but the guilt of his first sin; and this guilt is defined as an obligation to punishment: "This much misunderstood doctrine does not teach that Adam's sin was actually made ours. This consciousness repudiates. We know that we personally did not will it." Nor does it mean that we are to feel personally blameworthy for Adam's sin. Rather we simply participate in the legal consequences of his sin. His sin is ours in the sense that we are legally treated as he is on account of what he did by virtue of our legal union with him. This legal union has two grounds: first, the *natural* union with Adam as the root of all mankind; and, second, the *federal* relation instituted in him by God's covenant with him. Here we can see that Dabney parts company with Landis in favor of the view of Hodge.[50]

While the scripture nowhere explicitly says that Adam's sin was imputed to us, it clearly implies that such is the case. Since penal evils fall to the members of the race as a result of Adam's sin, the guilt of that sin must have been imputed to them. Moreover, man is in a condemned

---

48. Dabney, *Syllabus*, p. 220.

49. *Ibid.*, pp. 324 f., 327. For Dabney's argument as to how it can be just to hold men guilty for a state which is natural, see *Discussions*, pp. 273 ff.: "To this cavil we shall not now avert further than to approve the positions of Turretin and Hodge: That this corrupt estate, while not the result of an act of personal choice by us, is yet voluntary in the sense of being spontaneous; and that this being so, our reason always holds a moral agent meritorious for what he spontaneously is, without asking how he came to be such; as witness our judgments touching God, eternally and necessarily holy," etc.

50. *Ibid.*, p. 329.

state. Now either he was tried and found legally guilty in Adam, or has been condemned without a trial, a supposition unworthy of the divine Judge. Furthermore, the law of reproduction cannot account for this legal condition, as the Arminians teach. For that law cannot be justly extended to include moral relations if its operation has no judicial basis, namely the guilt of Adam. These conclusions are confirmed by the parallel presented in Romans 5 and I Corinthians 15. For if men are saved in Christ by the imputation of His righteousness, they must be lost in Adam by the imputation of his guilt.[51]

Dabney defends the federal arrangement as uniquely just on much the same ground as others before him.[52] Nevertheless, he admits that the grand objection of the Pelagians and skeptics of all ages is still repeated: "How can it be justice, for me, who gave no consent to the federal arrangement, for me, who was not present when Adam sinned, and took no share in it, save in a sense purely fictitious and imaginary, to be so terribly punished for another man's deed. This is nothing else than the intrinsic injustice of punishing an innocent man for the fault of the guilty."[53]

To this objection five separate solutions have been proposed. First, there is the *Wesleyan* solution which is repudiated as inimical to the doctrines of grace. Second, *Edwards'* speculative doctrine of arbitrary identity is dismissed as worthless. Then *Realism* as represented by Baird is repudiated on much the same grounds as did Hodge, or Thornwell before his switch of position. Next there is the scheme of *mediate imputation*, which is rejected as Arminianism in disguise in that it makes one's own subjective corruption the real ground of all the penal evils incurred by original sin. In addition it provides no just basis for the operation of the law of propagation in the sphere of moral relations. Moreover, it logically represents men as having an antecedent, depraved existence, at least for a moment, before they pass on that account under condemnation; whereas scripture represents them as beginning their per-

---

51. *Ibid.*, pp. 329-331.

52. See, for example, Jonathan Edwards, *Works*, Vol. I (10th ed.), London, 1865, p. 222 (from *The Great Christian Doctrine of Original Sin Defended*); also Joseph Bellamy, *Works*, Boston, 1850, pp. 224 ff. (from *True Religion Delineated*).

53. *Ibid.*, pp. 334-338.

sonal existence in a condemned as well as a depraved state.[54]

Finally, there is the opposite scheme of *immediate imputation* as held by Turretin and Hodge, in which the sovereign imputation of the legal guilt of an alien sin logically and causally precedes depravity of nature, which in turn brings the addition of personal guilt, which, along with actual sin, is the basis for condemnation. This position assumes an exact parallel between the communication of condemnation and justification.

Dabney's major attack on this position is, as intimated above, to reject the very distinction between mediate and immediate imputation. This distinction which needlessly aggravates the awful doctrine of original sin, should never have been made. Moreover, much like the doctrine of Placaeus it gives a false impression. It logically represents men as having an undepraved personal existence, at least for an instant, before they become depraved as a penal consequence of the imputation of Adam's sin. The drift of this scheme is that the infant soul is initially pure. But in point of fact men never have any personal existence but a depraved one. As they enter it condemned, so they enter it depraved.[55]

Moreover, the parallel between the various imputations is not exact. God may justly transfer guilt from one moral agent to another, but it does not follow that He will do this under any conditions whatever. Christ bore our guilt voluntarily, but infants receive the imputation of Adam's sin when incapable of assent to it. In addition, "The imputation of Adam's sin was a transaction of strict, judicial righteousness; and the other transaction was one of glorious, free grace. It may be praiseworthy to dispense blessings above the deserts of the beneficiaries; it cannot be other than injustice to dispense penalties beyond the deserts of the culprits."[56] Also, Hodge reasons in a circle in his interpretation of Romans 5:12 ff. He first claims that the correct interpretation of the passage demands an exact parallel between the two imputations, and then proceeds to defend his interpretation from his assumed premise.[57]

Furthermore, all agree that the imputation of Adam's guilt is based on a community of nature with him. But now the question is, To

---

54. *Ibid.*, p. 340 f.

55. *Ibid.*, pp. 341 f.

56. *Ibid.*, pp. 343 f.

57. *Ibid.*, p. 347; cf. Dabney, *Discussions*, p. 262.

what nature of Adam are we united, to his fallen or unfallen nature? Certainly not the latter; otherwise we should have personally pre-existed since before the fall. Consequently, we are naturally united only to Adam fallen in that he had already fallen before the existence of the race. There is no moral nature of Adam to which we could be naturally united but his fallen nature. But if this natural union is an essential ground of the imputation, the imputation cannot be antecedent to that subjective depravity of nature on which it is partially grounded.[58]

One particular evasion has been raised to blunt the force of this argument. It is alleged that we all had a federal existence before our personal existence. But if this is a reference to anything more than God's foreordination and foreknowledge, common sense refutes it, since only existing beings sustain actual relations. Just as the Confession says that although God did from all eternity decree to justify the elect, nevertheless they are not justified until their renewal by the Holy Spirit (XI, iv); so, in the same manner by parity of reasoning, although "God did, from all eternity, decree to condemn all men federally connected with Adam in his fall, nevertheless, they are not condemned actually, until they actually begin to exist in natural and federal union with their fallen head."[59]

Next Dabney argues, in the manner of Landis, that the supposition of an exact parallel between the imputation of Christ's righteousness and Adam's guilt undermines the doctrine of justification. The charge is that on the basis of this parallel (supposedly demanded by scripture), the view of Placaeus leads to the Roman view of justification on the ground of an inherent righteousness. But, argues Dabney, the doctrine of a justification parallel to immediate imputation would be something like this:

> The sinner, while still in his depravity, gets Christ's righteousness directly, gratuitously and antecedently, imputed to him; and then, as part of the consequent reward of that imputed merit, has regeneration wrought, infusing the sanctified nature of His redeeming Head into his soul. But as faith is in order to justification, this speculation must lead us to the following order. First, the convicted sinner, while unrenewed, exercises the initial saving faith. Second, he is thereupon justified. Third, he then procures, as one of the fruits of the

---

58. *Ibid.*, page 344; cf. *Discussions*, page 270.

59. *Ibid.*; cf. *Discussions*, pp. 270 f.

reconciliation, a holy heart, like his Savior's. Now, a moderate tincture of theology will teach any one that this is precisely the Arminian theory of justification. And a little reflection will show, that he who makes faith precede regeneration in the order of causation, must, if consistent, be a synergist. Thus it appears that this scheme cuts off the Calvinistic doctrine of justification as rigidly as it does Placaeus.[60]

The Calvinistic doctrine of justification teaches that the imputation of Christ's righteousness depends upon a spiritual union with him, and not vice versa: "In short, the believer is not justified in order to become a partaker of Christ's nature. He is made a partaker of Christ's nature in order to be justified. The vital union is both legal and spiritual: community in Christ's righteousness is one fruit; holy living is the other."[61]

Moreover, Hodge holds with all Calvinists that since one aspect of the ground of the imputation of Adam's guilt is natural union with him, the consequences of his fall, namely guilt and depravity, must come upon the race in the same order in which they occurred in him. In this connection, Dabney appeals to Edwards' insistence that the two elements must be in us just as they were in Adam, although he does not notice the latter's distinction between initial and confirmed depravity. He remarks, "Now common sense tells us, that when a holy creature committed his first sin, the depravation of his heart and the falling under guilt were, temporally speaking, synchronous; but that, causatively speaking, the depravation, or subjective corruption, must precede, and the guilt follow." Now if this was the case with Adam, who was not corrupted of God but of himself, how could it be any different with his posterity? Temporally, they are guilty when corrupted and corrupted when guilty; but causatively, to put first things first, they are guilty because corrupted rather than corrupted because guilty.[62]

In the end, Hodge simply dodges the objection that an imputation of Adam's sin, without our participation or consent in it, is intrinsically unjust. He simply says, God arranged it that way, therefore

---

60. *Ibid.*, p. 345.

61. *Ibid.*, pp. 345 f. By "holy living" here Dabney appears to mean progressive sanctification which is the result of the initial spiritual union with Christ and the definitive sanctification simultaneous with it.

62. Dabney, *Discussions*, p. 269; cf. *Syllabus*, p. 346.

it is just. But, affirms Dabney, if a thing is intrinsically wrong, nothing could make it right; and the man who claims that scripture teaches that God did such must be misinterpreting scripture and misrepresenting God: "Revelation is said to be accepted though it teaches mysteries entirely above reason. But it could not be accepted, if it taught inevitable contradictions, which are *against reason*. For no man could believe, were he to try, against those intuitive laws of thought which constitutes him a thinking and believing creature." We can be sure that God, however sovereign, will not act on a principle intrinsically wrong.[63]

Dabney is convinced that his own view, which is purported to be that of Calvin and holy scripture, is not, like Hodge's, liable to the criticism put forward by the Pelagian rationalists of all ages, simply because it takes the case out of the category of human justice, in which, if it really belonged there, its injustice would be readily self-evident. This view lifts the imputation of Adam's sin into a category all its own and wholly unique. Such uniqueness has two advantages. *First*, men reason by parallel instances, but in a case wholly unique, while they may not fully comprehend, they cannot convict of injustice. *Second*, the individual enters personal existence depraved and guilty. Not for one moment of his personal existence is he innocent. Thus he has no pretext to complain that he has been robbed of his personal innocence by imputation. For having never existed as an innocent person, he has no claims on divine justice.

An illustration is in order: Suppose a man is legally charged with a crime which he did not personally commit and to which he did not consent. His lawyer could argue that his innocence prior to the charge exonerates him from it. But the son of Adam has no such prior innocence because he has no personal existence prior to the imputation of Adam's sin. He does not approach the judicial issue as one innocently charged with guilt since as long as he has had personal existence he has been personally worthy of guilt.[64]

To bolster this argument, we might refer to Dabney's later disagreement with Landis, and the Realists as well, as to the meaning of Romans 5:12. To him the expression "all sinned" cannot refer to any actual sin committed before the individuals of the race existed. The verb

---

63. *Ibid.*, pp. 277 ff. Here we see Dabney turning Hodge's own principles against him.

64. *Ibid.*, pp. 279-281; cf. Dabney, *Syllabus*, pp. 349 f.

"sinned" refers to actual sin successively committed. Therefore, the apostle means to teach that all men, like Adam, personally sinned also. In this manner they endorse their first father's rebellion, and thus it is just for God to include them with him in a common guilt. From this it appears that Dabney, to try to make him consistent with what we have already seen of his position, is appealing to actual sin *both* as an indication that men do come into the world as guilty sinners *and* as a basis for the justice of their being charged with Adam's guilt. Whether these two assertions are consistent is a doubtful matter. At any rate, we can see Dabney's final attempt to include some notion of actual consent in his solution.[65]

It also appears from this later opinion that Dabney was not completely satisfied with his earlier solution. But this can be seen in the very presentation of his original solution. For instance, he writes:

> This dispensation of God, then, remains unique, without any parallel in human jurisprudence. It is solemn, mysterious, awful; but it is placed where it is impossible to convict it of injustice on God's part. That his exercise of his sovereignty in this strange dispensation is holy, righteous, benevolent, and wise, we have this sufficient proof; that he has given us his own Son, in free grace, to repair the mischiefs which human sin causes under the case. Let us remember, that the covenant of paradise was liberal, equitable, and splendidly beneficent in its own character. Its failure was exclusively man's and Satan's fault.[66]

For Dabney this dispensation in no way implies that God is the efficient cause of human depravity and guilt, but only the permissive cause. But suppose one should ask why God should institute such a dispensation:

> Why God should ordain such a federal union in his righteous sovereignty, which he foresaw would result in the determination of a depraved and condemned individual existence for a whole race of creatures, none should presume to speculate. We see that he has done

---

65. *Ibid.*, pp. 166 f. Dabney appeals to the use of the aorist to signify successive action as in Matt. 5:21, 27, 31, 33. This opinion shows itself with his review of Landis in 1884, some eleven to thirteen years after the general solution adopted in his *Syllabus* (1871) and review of Hodge (1873).

66. Dabney, *Syllabus*, p. 350.

so. We can only perceive this ground of propriety for it in the light of natural reason: that it appears to be the most natural constitution for a company of creatures united to a first parent by that tie of race and propagation which is so fundamental a feature of humanity.[67]

Finally, the Southern theologian wants it known that in this doctrine we are facing "an inscrutable providence"; that his particular view "leaves it enveloped in a mystery which the wisest and best of us most clearly see will never be solved in this world."[68]

Thus we see Dabney's manifold appeal in his defense of the doctrine, appeals which go beyond his own distinctive solution. He makes a New England-like appeal to concurrence with Adam's sin as manifested by actual transgression. He sounds somewhat Wesleyan in his appeal to the counterbalancing effects of God's grace. He appeals to the intrinsic justice of the federal constitution while at the same time appealing to its accord with natural reason and the natural union between Adam and the race. If this is not sufficient, Dabney knows from revelation that the God who has in fact ordained the natural and federal unions is just. Finally, his ultimate appeal is to the mystery of the matter.

What then is the justification for placing Dabney in the Agnostic "School"? Certainly, it is clear that he is not a slavish disciple of Landis by any stretch of the imagination. Moreover, his view has affinities with Calvin and Placaeus, with Edwards and Hodge, as well as with Breckinridge and Landis. The answer is simply this: *one,* there is no other category in which to place him. He is opposed to New School theology; he denies the very distinction between mediate and immediate imputation; he disagrees strongly with the distinctive view of the Princeton School; and he is adamantly opposed to any notion of Realism. And, *two,* he ultimately leaves the matter enveloped in mystery.

---

67. Dabney, *Discussions*, p. 281.
68. Dabney, *Syllabus*, p. 349.

V.
The Westminster School
John Murray

Westminster Theological Seminary was founded in 1929 as a protest against the inroads of a new liberal theology into the Presbyterian Church in general and into Princeton Seminary in particular. This liberal theology denied the very framework in which the problem of original sin had traditionally been set by its denial of the decisive authority of scripture, the historicity of Adam, and even the most rudimentary elements of the Biblical doctrine of original sin.[1] In opposition to this development it is the aim of Westminster, while differing somewhat in apologetic approach, to uphold the basic content of the old Princeton version of classic Reformed theology.

The Princeton School had, however, managed to maintain its distinctive doctrine of original sin intact. A. A. Hodge, who succeeded his father in the chair of systematic theology, held the latter's doctrine both in form and content.[2] He believed that the doctrine of federal representation as the ground of the infliction of original sin was the best explanation ever offered. To him "the Scriptural doctrine of the immediate and antecedent imputation of Adam's sin to his descendants, instead of being a repulsive and unnecessarily aggravated feature of Calvinism, is the most honouring to God and gratifying to the moral sense of men, of

---

1. Cf. H. S. Smith, *op. cit.*, pp. 192 ff. An example of this development is William Adams Brown, Professor of Systematic Theology at Union Seminary (N.Y.) 1898-1932.

2. See A. A. Hodge, *The Atonement,* Edinburgh, 1868, pp. 74 ff on the Federal Headship of Adam; and also *Outlines of Theology,* London, 1879, pp. 348 ff, "Imputation of Adam's First Sin."

all the solutions of the awful but undeniable facts of the case which have ever been attempted."[3] Whatever mystery still remains can only "lose itself in that abyss which is opened by the fact of the permission of sin, before which all schools of Theists on this side the veil must bow in silence."[4]

The son, however, did attempt to refine his father's doctrine in the face of some of the criticisms ranged against it. For instance, in answer to the charge that a gratuitous imputation of sin is both unthinkable and contrary to scripture, he wrote, "If the imputation of Christ's righteousness is immediate the imputation of Adam's sin must be the same, though the basis of the one is grace it is no less just, and though the basis of the other is justice, the original constitution from which it originated is no less gracious." This appears to amount to a modification of the older Hodge's position. At any rate, it shows that the force of the criticism against it was keenly felt.[5]

We may assume that the younger Hodge's successor, Benjamin B. Warfield, held what he termed the "Federalistic" view of the elder Hodge.[6] His successor in turn, Caspar W. Hodge, who held the chair of systematic theology at Princeton when Westminster was founded in 1929, espoused the same position.[7] The founder of the Westminster School, former Princeton professor J. Gresham Machen, did not profess to be original in his book, *The Christian View of Man,* but only to be popularizing the doctrines of the Hodges and Warfield.[8]

But Machen was not Professor of Systematic Theology at West-

---

3. A. A. Hodge, *Atonement,* p. 75; cf; p. 109.

4. A. A. Hodge, *Outlines of Theology,* p. 366.

5. *Ibid.,* p. 361. In this connection, it is evident that A. A. Hodge had read Dabney (p. 366). As far as the author knows, none of the Princeton theologians ever replied directly to Landis or Dabney.

6. Warfield, *op. cit.,* p. 308.

7. See article on "Imputation," *International Standard Bible Encyclopedia,* Vol. III, Grand Rapids, 1939, pp. 1462 ff .

8. J. Gresham Machen, *The Christian View of Man,* New York, pp. v f. (Preface). Cf. Machen's own statement of the doctrine of imputation (pp. 260 f.): "When the Bible teaches that Adam's first transgression was imputed to his descendants, that does not mean that those descendants had actually committed the first transgression. But the penalty which God pronounced upon the sin of Adam rested upon them. Adam committed that first transgression as their representative," etc.

minster. That position fell to John Murray, who, although a Scot, spent all his active teaching ministry in America. It is both interesting and significant that Murray should feel obliged to give the doctrine of original sin protracted study and treatment. His own formulation appears in *The Imputation of Adam's Sin,* together with the first volume of his commentary on *Romans,* both published in 1959. (Since the commentary appeals to the former work as a fuller statement of the author's position, we shall confine our exposition of Murray's position to it.)[9] The Westminster professor, apparently, was not satisfied with any of the Presbyterian formulations of the nineteenth century.

It is also significant, and typical of the Westminster professor, that he should attempt to be painfully careful to rest his formulation upon exegetical considerations alone. For instance, his chief interest is not to justify the doctrine of original sin, but simply to draw out the express meaning and implications of what Paul says in Romans 5. To this end, he is of course conversant with what his predecessors have said before him.

After a short discussion of the syntax of the passage, Murray addresses himself, in his work on the *Imputation of Adam's Sin,* to the crucial question as to the nature of the sin contemplated in the famous phrase of verse 12, "in that all sinned."[10] If, in general, sin and death entered humanity through the sin of the one man Adam, and if, more specifically, death passed upon all men due to the fact that all sinned, what is the precise nature of the sin of all?

The Pelagian view that Paul is referring to the voluntary, actual sin of all is roundly rejected on factual, exegetical, and theological grounds. *First,* it simply is not true, as in the case of infants, that all die because of their own individual acts of sin. Moreover, death is said to exercise its sway over those who did not sin as Adam did (5:13 f.). *Second,* on strictly exegetical grounds it must be recognized that Paul explicitly says that death reigns over all by the *one* trespass of the *one* man Adam (5:15-19). And, *third,* the Pelagian exegesis violates the theology

---

9. John Murray, *The Imputation of Adam's Sin,* Grand Rapids, 1959; cf. *The Epistle To the Romans,* Vol. I, Grand Rapids, 1959, pp. 178 ff. This appeal (p. 180, n. 17) is actually to a series of articles by the same name which originally appeared in the *Westminster Theological Journal* and were later published in book form.

10. *Ibid..* pp. 9 ff. So Murray translates ἐφ ᾧ πάντες ἥμαρτον.

of the sustained parallelism which the passage posits between condemnation through Adam and justification through Christ. For were the Pelagian interpretation true, it would mean that just as men are condemned solely by their own evil works, in the same manner they are justified by their own good works, a doctrine inimical to Paul's teaching in this immediate context.

Likewise Murray rejects the Augustinian view of the Church of Rome, and Calvin, that Paul means that all sinned in the sense that all have been imbued with original sin, or natural corruption; that is, all have been corrupted in Adam. The arguments against this exegesis are: first of all, the presumptive argument that it is difficult to conceive how the historical aorist ($\H{η}μαρτον$) could be used to refer to the constant process of hereditary corruption.[11] Then, again, how could the notion of death on account of original corruption comport with Paul's express statement that death is through the one sin of the one man Adam? Finally, the Augustinian interpretation implies, on the basis of the theological parallelism put forward by the apostle, a Romish view of justification. For if condemnation is by the hereditary transfusion of original sin, then justification, to preserve the parallelism, must be by the infusion of righteousness.

Against the former interpretations, Murray opts for what he calls "the Classic Protestant interpretation."[12] He prefaces his argument for this position with the following exegetical considerations: *one,* it is clear that Paul teaches that all die because "all sinned"; *two,* it is at the same time likewise clear that all die because one man, namely Adam, sinned; *three,* since the apostle cannot be dealing with two different facts when he mentions on the one hand the sin of all men (5:12), and on the other the one sin of the one man (5:15-19), he must be referring to one

---

11. This argument would have little cogency if the $πάντες\ \H{η}μαρτον$ were taken to mean that all sinned in the sense that all corrupted themselves in the Adamic sin, when he first sinned — as well it might be taken within the framework of Augustinian tradition.

12. Apparently, from the ensuing discussion in the book, this means the view that all sinned representatively in Adam, or that all are considered to have sinned when Adam their representative sinned. But it must be noted that Murray does not at this point in his discussion (pp. 19-21, "The Classic Protestant Interpretation") or later, explicitly state what is precisely the Classic Protestant interpretation. We can only assume that it amounts to his own position, which is apparently equated with it.

and the same sin: "The one event or fact can be expressed in terms of both singularity and universality."[13]

Therefore, the basic question to be answered is: On what basis can Paul say that "all sinned," and that the one sin can still be referring to the same fact? It is maintained that, in answering this question, we must not tone down either the singularity or the universality of the sin contemplated, since Paul clearly speaks of both: "The only solution is that there must be some kind of solidarity existing between the 'one' and the 'all' with the result that the sin contemplated can be regarded at the same time and with equal relevance as the sin of the 'one' or as the sin of 'all.'"[14]

When we search the scriptures, we find the fact of racial solidarity everywhere apparent. But this fact does not settle the question as to its precise nature. It is true that the scriptures do teach a natural or seminal union between ancestor and progeny, as for instance between Abraham and Levi (Heb. 7:9 f). According to this conception, Adam was the "natural root" of all mankind, and his sin was attributable to the race on this basis.[15] Exegetes and theologians, however, have not been content, and rightly so, to rest the imputation of Adam's sin upon this seminal union alone, but have cast about for some additional solidarity to serve as a sufficient ground for the involvement of the race in Adam's first sin.[16]

---

13. *Ibid.,* pp. 19-21.

14. *Ibid.,* p. 21.

15. In this connection the Westminster Confession (VI, iii), without appeal to the notion of a covenant representation, or even a covenant of works, simply states (as has been noted in the Introduction above): "They [i.e., Adam and Eve] being the root of all mankind, the guilt of this sin [i.e., Adam's first sin] was imputed, and the same death in sin and corrupted nature conveyed, to all their posterity, descending from them by ordinary generation." The Larger Catechism, however, appeals to a covenant of works as the ground of the imputation (Q. 22; cf. The Shorter Catechism, Q. 16). Murray notes these facts on p. 38, n. 56.

16. Murray, *op. cit.,* pp. 23 f. (cf. p. 34): "They have been constrained to posit some solidaric relationship other than the genealogical as necessary to a proper grounding of the involvement in Adam's sin, whether this additional relationship is conceived of as co-ordinate with the genealogical or as in itself the specific ground of the imputation of Adam's first sin." On the other hand (p. 23), "It may not be alleged that the fact of seminal relationship is irrelevant in this connection. We may not presume to say that the solidarity of the race with Adam, by reason of which all are involved

At this point Murray examines the Realistic view of Shedd and others that human nature was numerically and specifically one in Adam, and rejects it as an inadequate explanation. For *one* thing, it does not relieve the difficulty arising from the question as to how the individual members of the race can be guilty of a sin which they did not, as individuals, personally commit; for that they did not individually and personally participate in Adam's sin the Realist is obliged to admit.[17] *Secondly,* the theological analogy of Romans 5:12 ff. precludes the Realistic construction of the union; for all admit there is no realistic union subsisting between Christ and the justified, which the sustained parallelism of the passage would demand if Realism were true. *Third,* there is no scriptural evidence for any Realistic union above and beyond that which is contemplated in seminal union of nature.[18]

Furthermore, the contention that only Realism lays an adequate foundation in justice for the imputation of Adam's sin, whereas imputation on the basis of any sort of representative union would be a travesty of justice, is without foundation. For scripture teaches that genuine moral responsibility hinges upon corporate relationships in which realistic union is clearly not involved. In Murray's words:

> Moral responsibility devolves upon the members of a corporate entity by virtue of the actions of the representatives or the representative of that entity. Consequently the denial of the imputation of vicarious sin runs counter to the way in which the principle of solidarity operates in other spheres. And it is not valid to insist that vicarious

---

in his sin, could have been true if he had not been the father of all mankind. Whatever additional principle of solidarity may be posited or established it cannot be abstracted from the fact of biological ancestry."

17. *Ibid.,* pp. 32 f.; Murray is here replying to Shedd's charge that the notion of the imputation of sin on the basis of a representative union with Adam would be "an arbitrary act of sovereignty." Note the following comment: "The sin of generic humanity is just as far removed from the individual sin of the members of posterity as is the sin of a representative head and that for the simple reason that *as individuals* posterity did not yet exist. In other words, it is as difficult to establish the nexus between the sin of generic humanity and the members of the race as it is to establish the nexus between the sin of Adam as representative head and the members of the race. After all, generic humanity as it existed in Adam is impersonal, unindividualized human nature."

18. *Ibid.,* pp. 33-35.

sin can be imputed only when there is the *voluntary* engagement to undertake such imputation. Corporate relationship [e.g,. that existing within the state] exists by divine institution and the corporate responsibilities exist and come to effect apart altogether from voluntary engagement on the part of the persons concerned to assume these responsibilities. It is only because we fail to take account of the pervasiveness of corporate responsibility and think too lightly of the implications of this responsibility that we might be ready to accede to the argument that there cannot be the imputation to us of the sin of a vicarious representative. As the principle applies to Adam it is not difficult to see that imputation of sin on the basis of Adam's representative capacity could operate with unique and universal application. For this would be but the extension to the whole race, in terms of its solidarity in Adam, of a principle which is exemplified constantly in more restricted corporate relationships.[19]

As already apparent, the Westminster School espouses the representative view of the union subsisting between Adam and the race. Before presenting the arguments for this view, Murray is careful to emphasize that it does not deny, but rather strongly affirms the natural headship of Adam, the seminal union with him involving a community of nature, the corruption of that nature in Adam, and the propagation by natural generation of a corrupt human nature from him to all his posterity: "On the representative construction natural headship and representative headship are correlative, and each aspect has its own proper and specific function in the explanation of the status and condition in which the members of the race find themselves in consequence of their relation to Adam."[20]

---

19. *Ibid.,* pp. 35 f..

20. *Ibid.,* pp. 37 f. (cf. pp. 26 f). Murray continues, "Hence it must be appreciated that emphasis upon the natural headship of Adam and upon the seminal union of Adam and his posterity in Reformed theologians is not to be interpreted as vacillation between two incompatible ideas, nor is appeal to natural headship and seminal relationship on the part of such theologians to be regarded as the espousal of the realist construction" (p. 38). Note also the following delineation of the issue between the two views: "Hence the crux of the question is not whether the representative view discounts seminal union or natural headship or community of nature in that unity which exists between Adam and posterity but simply and solely whether the necessary *plus* which both views posit is to be interpreted in terms of an entity which existed in its totality in Adam and is individualized in the members of the race or in terms of a re-

The scriptural arguments for the representative view may be summarized as follows: First of all, since "there is something severely unique and distinct about our involvement in the sin of Adam" in that we are said to be accountable for that *one* sin of his, and since seminal union cannot explain why that first sin alone is imputed to us, we must conclude that some additional factor is necessary to explain why the apostle restricts our involvement in the penal consequences of Adam's sin to his first sin alone:

> In the light of the narrative in Genesis 2 and 3 we have to infer that the prohibition of the tree of the knowledge of good and evil was associated with and epitomized some special relationship that was constituted by divine institution and by reason of which the trespass or disobedience of Adam in this particular involved not only Adam but all of his posterity by natural generation. In other words, there was a special act of providence by which a special relationship was constituted in terms of which we are to interpret the implications for posterity of that one trespass of Adam in partaking of the forbidden fruit.[21]

Next, Murray appeals to the comprehensive analogy between Adam and Christ: "And since that analogy is so conspicuous, it is surely necessary to assume that the kind of relationship which Christ sustains to men is after the pattern of the relationship which Adam sustains to men." But natural headship is not analogous to the relationship between Christ and His people. Hence whatever union subsists between Adam and the race, so as to result in the imputation of his sin, must be in addition to natural union.[22]

Now then we know that the union between Christ and the justified is one of vicarious representation. Therefore, we may legitimately assume that the union between Adam and posterity is also one of vicarious representation. Moreover, we are explicitly told that Adam is the type of Christ, and therefore can assume that the sin, condemnation, and death proceeding from his one sin came to men after a pattern identical to that by which righteousness, justification, and life proceed to men from the singular sacrificial obedience of Christ. Murray is here

---

presentation which was established by divine ordination. It is on that restricted question that the debate must turn" (p. 27).

21. *Ibid.,* p. 39.

22. *Ibid.*, pp. 39 f.

obviously reasoning from the status of the antitype (Christ) to the status of the original type (Adam).

Thus we cannot posit anything less than a union of vicarious representation between the race and Adam, and it would be foolish to posit anything more since there is no scriptural evidence or demand for it: "When we seek to discover the specific character of the union which will ground the imputation of Adam's first sin we find it to be that same kind of union as is analogous to the union that exists between Christ and His people and on the basis of which His righteousness is theirs unto justification and eternal life. How we should denominate this kind of union is a matter of terminology. If we call it representative union or headship, this will suffice for identification purposes."[23] We may add that Murray significantly does not speak in terms of a *federal,* or covenant, union.

The Westminster theologian then turns to the nature of the imputation of Adam's sin. After an extended historical discussion of the various opinions of his predecessors, he concludes that "the mode by which the sin of Adam comes to be reckoned to posterity must be stated and resolved in terms of the antithesis between mediate and immediate imputation as that antithesis had been sharply defined in the Placaean debate of the seventeenth century." Thus we note that Murray, unlike Dabney, accepts the validity of the distinction put forward by Placaeus, and puts forward his view in terms of it. As might be expected, he is, following in the tradition of the Princeton School, a pronounced advocate of immediate imputation.[24]

The question, then, is whether our involvement in Adam's first sin is based directly on our judicial relationship to him as our representative, or whether it is mediated through the inheritance of a corrupt nature from him. The exegetical data of Romans 5 demand that the involvement must be immediate. Briefly summarized, it demands, first, the immediate conjunction of the sin of Adam and the *death* of all; second, the immediate conjunction of the sin of Adam and the *condemnation* of all; and, third, the immediate conjunction of the sin of Adam and the *sin* of all. It is evident that representative solidarity is an immediate solidarity which

---

23. *Ibid.,* p. 41.
24. *Ibid.,* pp. 63, 64 ff.

renders unnecessary any mediating instrument.[25]

Furthermore, the analogy between justification and condemnation precludes mediate imputation. For if justifying righteousness comes to believers through no other medium than that of judicial union with Christ (that is, it is not mediated through righteousness inwrought in regeneration and sanctification), it follows that condemning sin should come to unbelievers through no other medium than that of judicial union with Adam — that is, if the analogy of Romans 5 is to hold. In other words, mediate imputation, in terms of the analogy, implies the Romish view of justification, which is exactly what Paul is combating in this passage.[26] It is very obvious that at this point Westminster is closely following the exegesis and argumentation of Princeton.

But if all sinned in Adam, how are we to define this sin of all in the sin of Adam? What is the nature of the sin imputed to posterity? Thus the question raised is, "What was reckoned in the divine judgment as having occurred in the case of posterity when Adam fell? God's judgment is always according to truth, and what he reckoned as having occurred actually did occur. The question is then: what did happen? And this is to say: what was imputed to posterity?"[27]

We may notice that the axiom, reminiscent of such theologians as Baird and Landis, that "God's judgment is always according to truth" influences the very formulation of the question; and may presume that Murray rejects the distinctive view of Hodge that all that is imputed is the judicial obligation to satisfy justice which is indeed the case. Hodge's

---

25. *Ibid.*, pp. 64-67. *Ibid.*. pp. 64-67. For instance, note this comment, on Rom. 5:18 concerning the relationship between the one sin of Adam and the condemnation of all: "This is an unambiguous assertion to the effect that the ground, or, if we will, the medium, of the condemnation of all is the one trespass of Adam. To intrude the medium of inherited depravity would introduce another factor, namely, another sin or aspect of sinfulness, which would plainly violate the emphasis that it was from the *one trespass* that the judgment of condemnation came upon all. In other words, the interjection of inherited depravity, which, on the premises of mediate imputation, is the crucial and explanatory consideration, posits an addition which is palpably inconsistent with the apostle's emphasis upon the singularity of the trespass from which universal condemnation proceeded. This is just saying that no other sin or aspect of sinfulness can be allowed to interfere with the conjunction of the one trespass of Adam and the condemnation of all. And this means immediate conjunction" (p. 67).

26. *Ibid.*, p. 70.

27. *Ibid.*, p 72.

view is rejected on the following grounds:

Exegetically, Paul teaches that we are involved not only in the judicial consequences of the sin of Adam, but in the sin itself. He explicitly says that "all sinned" and "were constituted sinners" (Romans 5:12, 19). Moreover, it is not clear that to be counted a sinner in the usage of scripture can be reduced to the notion of obligation to satisfy justice.[28]

The chief *theological* objection is based on the Pauline analogy between justification and condemnation. For if in justification in Christ we do not receive merely the judicial benefit of His righteousness, but that righteousness itself, just so in condemnation in Adam we are not merely involved in the judicial liability of his sin, but in the sin itself. On the other hand, Hodge's appeal to the analogy of the vicarious sin-bearing of Christ will not do in the light of the sublime uniqueness of the work of the Savior.[29]

Then there is an *historical* objection, namely the consideration that the classical Reformed and Lutheran theologians never separated liability to punishment *(reatus pœnæ)* from liability to blame *(reatus culpæ)*. They held the one to be inconceivable apart from the other. We not only suffer for Adam's sin, but are really to blame for it.[30] The reasoning behind this traditional position comports with Murray's own: "To impute penal liability without the imputation of that to which the penal liability is due is faced with a juridical objection. Although it is not ours to solve all mysteries and by no means ours to call in question the government of God in inflicting the whole race with the penal consequences of Adam's own sin, yet we have no need or right to complicate the mystery by making the kind of disjunction which the notion of the mere imputation of judicial liability entails."[31] Thus we see that there is also, in

---

28. *Ibid.*, p 74 f.

29. *Ibid.*, pp. 76-78; cf. pp. 93-94.

30. *Ibid.*, pp. 78 ff. The evidence for this contention is voluminous. The Reformed theologians followed the doctrine of Calvin: "There is no *reatus* without *culpa* (*Institutio*, II, i, 8). Cf. the comment of J. Braun: "So *reatus* is something midway between fault and punishment *(medium quid inter culpam et pœnam)*. It arises from fault and leads to punishment, so that there is but a single *reatus culpæ* and *reatus pœnæ*.... Where there is no *culpa*, no *reatus* and no *pœna* is conceivable at all." Heppe, *Dogmatics*, p. 326. For the Latin, see the German edition: *Die Dogmatik der Evangelisch-Reformierten Kirche* (ed. E. Bizer), Neukirchen, 1958, p. 265.

31. *Ibid.*, p. 85.

Murray's own terms, a *judicial* objection to the doctrinal construction of Hodge.

Up to this point, the discussion of the question under consideration has been basically negative. However, the Westminster theologian must not simply refute Hodge's answer, but come up with an answer of his own. To this end, he summarizes the positive fruit of the negative discussion with respect to the Princeton School as follows:

> Out of deference to the biblical teaching we shall have to recognize and make allowance for a real involvement on our part in Adam's sin that is not to be construed as actual, voluntary participation or the *transfer* of moral character, on the one hand, and yet is not to be reduced to the level of judicial liability, on the other. We must insist on the involvement of posterity in Adam's sin in a way that will place this involvement in the category of sin and yet maintain that it was Adam's trespass in a manner that is not ours. In the language of theology we must try to do justice to both considerations, that, in respect of posterity, Adam's trespass was both *peccatum alienum* and *peccatum proprium.*[32]

The question remains: What is involved in the imputation of Adam's first sin so as to make it truly an imputation of sin, and not merely of the judicial liability of sin? It is the question as to the relationship between the depravity of Adam's first sin in which we all participate, and the imputation of that one sin to posterity.[33]

In attacking this question, Murray again appeals to the analogy between justification and condemnation. Just as believers are "constituted righteous," in the exact same way all men must have been "constituted sinners." Thus while it is the sphere of the forensic that is contemplated in both cases, it is an actual obedience and disobedience that is imputed in both cases: "Viewed from the standpoint of personal, voluntary action the disobedience in the one case is that of Adam and the obedience is that of Christ. But the effect of the constituting act is that

---

32. *Ibid.*, p. 86.

33. *Ibid.*, pp. 86, 90, 92 ("the question of the relation of depravity to the imputation of the trespass of Adam"). It is the old question as to the relationship between our participation in the *depravity* of Adam's first sin on the one hand, and our participation in its *guilt* on the other.

others, not personally and voluntarily engaged, come to have property, indeed propriety, in the personal, voluntary performance of another. It is both *alienum* and *proprium,* and neither aspect must be stressed to the exclusion of the other." So that we can say that "the sin of Adam is reckoned to be as really and properly ours as is the righteousness of Christ in justification."[34]

This may be all we can say on the authority of scripture. But it may be both profitable and not without warrant to pursue the question still further on the basis of the revealed analogy between our relationship to Christ on the one hand and to Adam on the other. At any rate, we know that there is more to solidarity with Christ and solidarity with Adam than the forensic aspect of that solidarity. So that we may assume that "as representative solidarity with Christ in his obedience unto death and in his resurrection secures and insures subjective renewal in regeneration, so representative solidarity with Adam in his sin involved for posterity their subjective depravity as well as the forensic judgment of their being 'constituted sinners.'"[35]

It is on the ground of this consideration that Murray puts forth his distinctive thesis in answer to the question as to the nature of the sin imputed to posterity: The imputation of Adam's sin carries with it, not merely as consequence but as implicate, the depravity with which all the members of the race begin their existence as distinct individuals.[36] In elucidation and elaboration of this thesis, we may note the following: first, that "depravity may not be conceived of so much as a penal infliction arising from the imputation of Adam's sin but as an implicate of solidarity with Adam and his sin."[37] In other words, representative solidarity with Adam involves identification with him not only in his overt act of sin, but also in the depraved attitude which is an inseparable concomitant of that act. Such an attitude is included in the very nature of the sin of Adam imputed to posterity, and thus belongs to them by virtue of their judicial solidarity with him. It is by imputation not only his evil disposition, but theirs. The depravity with which the race is inflicted is not the penal result of the imputation of Adam's sin, but is ra-

---

34. *Ibid.,* p. 88.

35. *Ibid.,* p. 89.

36. *Ibid.,* p. 92.

37. *Ibid.,* p. 90.

ther involved in the very imputation itself: "Our involvement in and identification with the sin of Adam carries with it as a necessary ingredient the pravity or perversity apart from which sin does not exist."[38] It is what Murray earlier designated in his exposition of Edwards "the *disposition* which is an integral element of the sin imputed."[39]

Next, on this view, while posterity cannot be conceived of as existing when Adam sinned, yet they were contemplated in the mind of God as foreordained to exist, and as thus contemplated they were only ever contemplated as in solidaric union with Adam and thus as having sinned in him, never as *potentially* one with Adam but always as *actually* one with him. Therefore, it is a mistake to ask when each individual member of the race becomes a depraved sinner, for no person ever exists as anything other than sinful. No one ever exists, or is conceived by God to exist, as pure and undefiled by sin. Each person is eternally contemplated by God as sinful by reason of his solidarity with Adam, and, whenever he comes to be, he comes to be as sinful: "Sinfulness is correlative with his beginning to be as an individual in his mother's womb." Likewise, the imputation of Adam's sin is correlative with one's beginning to be. In view of Adamic solidarity, sin is involved in his very exis-

---

38. *Ibid.*, p. 92.

39. *Ibid.,* p. 62. It should be noted that Murray basically follows Edwards at this point, at least his understanding of Edwards expressed in these words: "He [i.e., Edwards] is saying that by the divine constitution there is imputed to posterity the sin of Adam *both as evil disposition and overt action"* (p. 61). But at the same time it appears that he does not follow Edwards exactly. For the latter makes a clear-cut distinction between that *initial corruption,* or depravity, which is an integral element of the Adam's first sin, a disposition belonging both to him and his posterity, and that *confirmed,* or hereditary, *corruption* inhering in both as the result of their involvement in the first sin; and while it is true that it is all the same depravity, whether considered in one sense or the other, nevertheless it is the former which is involved in the imputation of Adam's sin, and the latter which as the penal result of that imputation is to be considered as distinct from it. So the doctrine of Edwards seems to be. Murray on the other hand, while recognizing the genius of this distinction between initial and confirmed depravity (pp. 57 ff), does not appear to employ it at all in elucidating the content of the imputation of Adam's sin. On this view it seems that it is the depravity of sin as such, as involved in exemplary fashion in the first sin, that is an integral element in the nature of that sin as imputed to posterity. This observation would appear to be confirmed by Murray's rejection of the view of both Edwards and Hodge that hereditary depravity is inflicted upon the race as the penal result of the imputation of Adam's sin.

tence.[40]

Finally, we do not become depraved by natural generation. Nor is natural generation the reason why we are conceived in sin: "The *reason* why we are naturally generated in sin is that, whenever we begin to be, we begin to be as sinful because of our solidarity with Adam in his sin. Thus the relation of natural generation to depravity is that by the former we begin to be and having begun to be we are necessarily sinful by reason of our involvement in Adam's sin. Natural generation we may speak of, if we will, as the means of conveying depravity, but, strictly, natural generation is the means whereby we come to be and depravity is the correlate of our having come to be."[41] Thus we have the position of the Westminster School as represented by Professor Murray. In summary, it is clear that it is a distinctive position in the history of the debate on the doctrine of original sin in American Presbyterian theology. For, in the first place, it will have nothing to do with New School Theology and mediate imputation. Moreover, while holding much in common, such as the doctrines of representative union and immediate imputation, it cannot be identified with the distinctive view of the Princeton School. For Murray — in the face of the severe criticism of Baird, Landis, and Dabney — demurs from Hodge at three points: *one,* he refuses to call the representative union a federal, or covenant, union; *two,* he emphatically rejects the doctrine that the race is only liable to the judicial penalty *(pœna)* of Adam's first sin, holding rather that all men really participate in its guilt *(culpa)*; and, *three,* he does not hold that hereditary depravity is the penal consequence of the imputation of Adam's sin.[42]

---

40. *Ibid.*, pp. 90 f. It would appear that this position is adopted, at least partially, in conscious reaction to Dabney's charge that Hodge's view of immediate imputation implies logically that men have some sort of depraved personal existence before they are penally inflicted with hereditary depravity; as well as to his discussion of the view that the race had a federal existence before the personal existence of the various individuals in it. See the discussion of Dabney's position above.

41. *Ibid.*, pp. 92 f.

42. Apparently, Murray does not agree with Landis that Hodge holds to what the former calls a "gratuitous" imputation (it is noteworthy that Hodge himself never uses the term) of Adam's sin. For he says in a footnote, referring to Landis' book, "This lengthy monograph is devoted to a large extent to criticism of Dr. Hodge's position, and particularly of what Landis calls the gratuitous imputation of Adam's sin to the race, a *position which he considers to be that of Hodge"* (*ibid.,* p. 83, italics added). It should also be noted that the reason why Murray refuses to call the representative

Furthermore, the view of Murray explicitly rejects the distinctive position of the Realistic School. And while sharing much in the spirit of the Agnostic School — for instance in its rest in the just, if mysterious, judgment of God — it cannot be subsumed under the agnosticism of Landis, for it does claim to set forth the precise mode of our participation in Adam's first sin. Nor does it agree with the distinctives of Dabney, particularly his rejection of the distinction between mediate and immediate imputation.

The Westminster School, thanks to John Murray, has a view all its own.[43]

---

union a "covenant" union is due to his inability to find in what he calls the "Adamic Administration" the elements of the Biblical notion of a divine covenant.

43. It should be noted at this point that the expression "Westminster School" is here used, for purposes of simplification, to refer to Murray's distinctive position, without intending to imply that this position is binding upon his former colleagues or successors on the faculty of Westminster Theological Seminary.

Conclusion
Analysis of the Various Viewpoints

It now remains for us to analyze and evaluate this most fascinating debate in American theological history. In doing so, we shall attempt, first, to set forth an interpretative summary of the issues, background, and course of the debate; and then, against the background of this historical summary, pass judgment upon the various viewpoints of the theologians involved — all with a view to a better understanding of the nature of the problems raised in the history of the debate.

Before we do so, however, it would be well to pause for the purpose of registering one's respect for the men who took part in this profound discussion. Regardless of one's own sentiments with respect to the issue at hand, one is obliged to recognize the theological greatness of these divines who made bold to attempt to deal with so great a question. For given the awesome character of the problem before them — and considering the forcefulness of the opposition to the doctrine of original sin which was their lot to face — our admiration of their noble and courageous attempts to solve it knows no bounds. If this debate on original sin signifies nothing else, it demonstrates that the American Presbyterian Church has a noble theological heritage which ought not to be despised — either by neglect in favor of Reformation and classical Reformed theology on the one hand, or by infatuation with so-called "modern" theology on the other.

We might also pause to mention certain general observations concerning the debate. There is, for one thing, its historical importance with respect to American history in general and the history of American Presbyterianism in particular. With regard to the former, there is little doubt that this debate on original sin was one of the most significant debates in American theological history in that it was a phase of one of the most fundamental conflicts inherent in the American heritage. It was an aspect of the conflict between humanistic American optimism on the one hand and the miserable-sinner Christianity of genuine American Calvinism on the other. Although this point could be developed at length, this is not the occasion to do so. At any rate, this same fundamental conflict which erupted initially in New England spread to Presbyterianism. It was the intention of all the principals in our debate to stem the tide of this humanism by means of their particular approaches to the doctrine of original sin.[1]

Another observation which pertains to the subject matter of the debate is simply this: the immense and often overwhelming complexity of the issue under discussion. This fact is particularly demonstrated by the maddening confusion of terms as they are used by the various disputants. For instance, one term may mean one thing in the theological expression of one man, and quite another in the terminology of another.[2]

Now in view of this manifold complexity, can we simplify the various issues in the debate for the purpose of the analysis and evaluation of it?

It would appear that the issues boil down to two basic questions: *one,* what is the mode of the union, or solidarity, between Adam and the race? And, *two,* what is the justice of the imputation of Adam's sin to the race? The thought content of these questions could be expressed and elaborated in different ways (as for instance in the Introduction above and in the discussions of the various theologians), but for our purposes we may allow them to express the heart of the issues at hand. It is obvious that these two questions are closely related and, upon further reflection, that one's answer to the second depends upon one's answer to the first. Thus the two may be blended into one, as follows: What is the nature of that moral connection, indeed union, between Adam and the

---

1. In this connection one might possibly argue that, the internecine strife among these theologians unintentionally contributed to the triumph of liberal theology and thus to the ascendancy of that very humanistic optimism which it was their intention to oppose. For this debate on original sin may well have contributed to that latitudinarian attitude toward doctrine which served as such a convenient occasion for the intrusion of modernism into the Church. For an account of the development of latitudinarianism in the case of the Presbyterian Church, U.S.A., see L. A. Loetscher. *The Broadening Church,* Philadelphia, 1954.

2. A good example is the divergent usage of the term "moral" on the part of Hodge and Landis; the former refers it to the criminal aspect of sin (*reatus culpæ*) whereas the latter uses it to refer to the federal connection or judicial aspect *(reatus pænæ).*

race which renders the race, taken both collectively and individually, justly participant in the guilt of his first sin and the depravity resulting from it? In other words, how is it both possible and just for it to be declared in scripture that all sinned in Adam: that is, that all men sinned when the first man committed the first sin?

In the light of this delineation of the problem, it can be seen that the most crucial matter under debate is the nature of our *moral* connection with Adam. For the justice of the imputation of Adam's first sin naturally depends on the justice of whatever *moral* solidarity subsists between the progenitor of the race and his progeny. The question thus boils down to the full and exact meaning of the scriptural expression "in Adam" (ἐν τῷ᾽ Ἀδάμ)³ – an expression which obviously refers to some sort of solidarity between the first man and his posterity.

Now as to the mode of our being in Adam, all the participants in the debate, in view of their common theological heritage, have a ready answer. It was well expressed, long before the debate, in the words of Jonathan Dickinson quoted above, "We are guilty, not merely as Descendants from Adam; but as being *naturally,* as well as *legally,* in him when he violated the first Covenant."⁴ Here in this statement we see manifested the twofold character of our solidarity with Adam. There is a *natural* union on the one hand, and a *legal* union on the other.

One can readily see, from the preceding account of the debate, that it is right at this point that the issues arise. The whole discussion revolves around those questions which relate to how one is to understand the precise character of, *one,* the natural union with Adam; *two,* the legal union with Adam; and, *three,* the relationship between the two.

First, how is one to conceive of the *natural* union or natural headship of Adam? The scriptures clearly indicate that there is a very real *seminal* union between ancestor and progeny. But in the case of whatever natural solidarity subsists between Adam and his posterity, is there some sort of *realistic* union in addition to this physical union? Further, is there some sort of *moral* relationship inhering in the natural union, so as to explain the propagation of hereditary depravity by means

---

3. 1 Corinthians 15:22. Cf. also Romans 5:12, where ἐφ᾽ ᾧ may possibly mean "in whom" (i.e., in Adam) and thus be the equivalent of ἐν τῷ Ἀδάμ.

4. Quoted from *The True Scripture-Doctrine Concerning Important Points of Christian Faith* (1741) by H. S. Smith, *op. cit.,* p. 6 (italics added). See above p. 14.

of it? Or does the natural relationship have no independent moral significance, that is, no moral significance except in close relationship to some
additional aspect of solidarity with moral significance?

This leads us, secondly, to the question of how one is to conceive of the *legal* — that is, judicial or forensic — union with Adam. In
precisely what sense is the race legally implicated in the guilt of what
Adam did? Are they guilty by virtue of some special covenant or federal
union with him in that God constituted him their federal head? And is
this judicial solidarity, whatever its precise nature, a union of representation? Moreover, does this legal union have any moral significance of
its own, or does its significance depend entirely on natural solidarity?

These inquiries naturally lead, third, to the question as to how
one is to conceive of the *relationship* between natural and legal solidarity. Are they independent or interdependent? If independent, in what
sense independent? And if interdependent, in what sense interdependent?
If, indeed, there is a close relationship between them, are they two separate relationships constituted by God or merely two aspects of one fundamental relationship existing in the very nature of the case? Furthermore, if they are mutually interdependent, are they equally interdependent, or is there a primary dependence of one upon the other? And if the
latter, which one is prior to the other? Is the natural dependent upon the
legal, or the legal upon the natural?

With this discussion of the problem in mind, let us now pass on
to summarize the historical background and course of the debate.

We have, first, as an essential element in the background of all
discussion, what may be called the Biblical realism of Augustine. This
is not to imply that Augustine's thinking on the subject may not have
been influenced somewhat by Greek realistic modes of thought, but
simply to maintain that the formative thrust in his approach was Biblical
in content while recognizing that his expression of that content often
assumes those neo-Platonic thought forms which served as perhaps the
most readily available form of intellectual expression in his day. According to Augustine, when God created the individual historical Adam, He
also created, in seminal form, that human nature from which every human being was to be propagated. In other words, when He created the
man Adam, He simultaneously created the race *mankind*. So when the
first man sinned, it was the race, including every individual to stem from
it, which really sinned, in that human nature corrupted itself in Adam.
Thus Augustine was preoccupied with our natural solidarity with Adam,

giving the legal relationship to him no independent discussion. He simply assumed that since God punishes all men with original sin, all are justly accounted guilty of Adam's apostasy on the basis of their natural kinship with him; otherwise God would be punishing them unjustly. That is, original corruption presupposes an original guilt. The legal relationship to Adam is secondary in the Augustinian approach, a mere corollary of the natural union.

The Scholastic theologians, as was customary with them, attempted to express their particular solution to the problem, if not their whole approach to its formulation and solution, in terms of whatever school of philosophy appealed to them. Thus we have the Augustinian solution expressed in the form of the Platonic Realism of Anselm and later in the more moderate Aristotelian Realism of Thomas. But Thomas' philosophical position forced him to look beyond a Realistic union of nature for some additional principle of solidarity, which, significantly, is a legal one suggested in political terms.[5] And when the later Nominalists were driven by their philosophical position to modify the Augustinian solution based upon the notion of natural solidarity, they sought to explain the doctrine of original sin more in terms of some sort of a legal relationship between Adam and the race which rendered it judicially liable to punishment for his first sin. The natural relationship to Adam, while recognized as the cause of original corruption, could not, on their view, be the just ground for our participating in the culpability of Adam's sin — a culpability which we do not in fact possess in that there cannot be, in reality, any such thing as a real human nature which, having sinned in Adam, is passed on to posterity so as to produce individual persons who are really sinful. Thus the Nominalists denied that men are born sinful by making our moral relationship to Adam consist solely in judicial terms.

In the face of this challenge, the Reformers in general, and Calvin in particular, reverted to the Biblical realism of Augustine. And though they gave much attention to the peculiarly forensic aspects of our union with Christ in salvation, they had little to say about the judicial aspects of our union with Adam in sin. It was the province of the classical Reformed Federal theology of the seventeenth century to develop this aspect of the doctrine of original sin.

---

5. See above, pp. 7 f., n. 12.

At this point it is important to recognize certain salient facts about the Federal theology. In the first place, the covenant theologians, unlike the Nominalist Catharinus who denied the Augustinian solution, *added* their conception of a covenant solidarity with Adam to the Augustinian conception of natural solidarity as it had been sanctioned by Calvin and his immediate followers. They simply added the concept of federal headship to that of natural headship. In the second place, in that the covenant theologians considered themselves, in general, the heirs of Augustine and Calvin, they saw no contradiction between covenant theology and the Augustinian tradition.[6] Third, there is the fact that the Federal theology did not arise full-blown, but was progressively restated during well over a century of development. This naturally means that there was to be development in the discussion of such questions as the nature of the covenant of works and its relationship to the natural union with Adam. For instance, there is little emphasis on the concept of a representative union in the earlier Reformed theology whereas this notion is a predominate one in the full-blown covenant theology of the latter half of the seventeenth century.

This factor leads us to the final observation that although the precise relationship between natural and legal solidarity was a matter of discussion and debate, as evidenced by the controversy over imputation, it was never definitely settled — unless one considers the *Formula Consensus Helvetica* (1675) a definitive settlement. But even so one finds its great defender, Turretin, sufficiently ambiguous that Hodge, on the one hand, and Landis and Baird, on the other, can appeal to him for support. It is simply a plain fact that classical Reformed theology is ambiguous at this specific point. There never was any consensus as to how one should conceive of the relationship between the two components of our twofold union with Adam. This fact is clearly illustrated by the

---

6. In this connection, it is significant that the foremost representatives of the Augustinian tradition in the Church of Rome were adamant opponents of the federal idea. This is especially true of Cornelius Jansenius, the foremost Augustinian, on all points, in the Roman communion, a man who read the writings of Augustine through seventeen times. Jansenius concluded that nothing could be more foreign and hostile to the spirit of Augustine's theology than the notion of God's making a covenant with Adam as the federal head of the human race. According to him, "All things take place by no agreement, but happen from the nature of things, because the children are said to have sinned in the parent and to have been one with him." Quoted from Jansenius, *Augustinus* (Louvain, 1640). Tom. II, p. 208, by Fisher, *History, op. cit,*. p. 352.

conspicuous ambiguity of the statement of Jonathan Dickinson quoted above, which may serve both as a summary conclusion to the broad historical background of the Presbyterian debate and as a fitting introduction to the debate itself.

But before discussing the debate itself, it is necessary to analyze the immediate occasion of it, namely, the attack on the moral and scriptural justification for the Federal view in the course of the eighteenth and early nineteenth centuries. The most influential of these attacks, that of John Taylor, came in 1741, the very year in which Dickinson's comment was published. There arose in response to this attack three approaches which greatly influenced the course of the Presbyterian debate. It is significant that all three of these were attempts to grapple with what was conceived to be a moral difficulty in the Federal view.

The first two of these responses came from the pen of those who were attempting to justify the *legal* arrangement upheld by the Federal theology. In other words, their motive was to defend the justice of the divinely constituted legal solidarity with Adam. For example, John Wesley justified it with an appeal to the Arminian doctrine of universal redemption. But the Wesleyan solution was not a live alternative for the strict Calvinism of Jonathan Edwards. Now it is evident that the motive behind Edwards' theory of identity was to justify the legal union with Adam with an appeal to the natural union. But with his theology of *personal* identity on the basis of an arbitrary divine constitution he transformed the traditional Augustinian notion of natural union – that is, the view that natural union consists in *racial* identity. Edwards' extreme Empiricism led him to adopt a fundamentally Nominalist view of our solidarity with Adam; but it was a Nominalist view of the *natural* union with Adam, not of the legal union – which distinguishes him from the Nominalists of the late middle ages. Furthermore, Edwards' Calvinism would not permit him to accept the traditional Nominalist view of the nature of original sin. At any rate, it is clear that the attempt was to ground the justice of the covenant arrangement in a union of nature.

It was the approach of the third response, that of the later New England theology, to deny altogether the covenant doctrine with both its Federal and Augustinian elements.[7] This denial found its way into the

---

7. It is a very interesting fact that the New England theologians did not, as far as the author knows, appeal to universal redemption in their attempt to justify our moral con-

Presbyterian Church by way of Albert Barnes and the more radical New School theologians. The whole of the debate within the Presbyterian Church must be understood in the light of the attempt to defend the Federal view from the radical New School attack.

This task fell first to the Princeton School in general, and to Charles Hodge in particular. Now it was the main contention of Hodge that while the necessity of the natural or seminal union must be maintained, the justice of our solidarity with Adam cannot be grounded upon any *natural* union with Adam, whether conceived of in Realistic or Edwardian terms. For, in the first place, it is a plain fact of consciousness and scripture that no such notion of identity, whether racial or personal, can either exist on the one hand or render the individuals of the race culpable for Adam's personal sin on the other. And, in the second place, the calamities resulting from Adam's first sin would not, on such a view, be penal in character, but simply natural consequences, or mere arbitrary impositions. If the justice of the connection with Adam were founded on the *natural* relationship alone, that would be a mere matter of sovereignty rather than a matter of justice. Therefore, the justice of the relationship must be founded upon the *legal* connection, namely, the federal arrangement.

Thus Hodge clearly subordinated the *natural* relationship to Adam to the *legal* relationship. While professing to be true to Augustine, he in effect expunged from the traditional Federal approach that fundamental Augustinian element which was originally such an integral part of it. That this is the case is clear from his denying that the individuals of the race are really culpable for Adam's first sin, though they are of course judicially liable to suffer punishment for it. And so while Hodge may not have been a Nominalist from the strictly philosophical standpoint, it is abundantly clear that, in his attempt to defend the Federal view in the face of the radical New School attack, he fell back into an essential element of the Nominalist doctrine. And while his strict Calvinism and exegetical acumen would not allow him to embrace the full-fledged doctrine of original sin, it is impossible to rescue him from the charge of Nominalism put so forcibly by R. W. Landis. He in

nection with Adam, although they accepted that doctrine. The question naturally arises as to why they chose to deny the federal doctrine altogether rather than justify it in the Wesleyan manner.

fact, if not in name, holds to the "gratuitous" imputation of Adam's personal sin.

There is also good reason to charge Hodge with ultimately falling back upon the Wesleyan doctrine of universal redemption. For in his attempt to escape the charge of Nominalism he maintains, following Calvin, that no man is finally condemned for Adam's sin alone (that is for a *peccatum alienum*) as the Nominalists taught, but also for his own inherent hereditary depravity. But Hodge further maintains, in order to defend his doctrine of universal infant salvation, that hereditary depravity is insufficient grounds for the final perdition of an individual. No one will ever be finally condemned who has no actual sins to atone for, that is, for original sin alone. On what basis, then, is such a person saved? By the gracious redemption of Christ, of course; there is no other way of salvation. But if every naturally born son of Adam is under condemnation, and if all these, except those who live to commit actual sin, are saved by the redemption of Christ, how can one escape the inference that Christ redeemed all except those who voluntarily reject that redemption by means of actual sin? Is not this, in principle, the doctrine of Wesley and Henry B. Smith that God has mitigated the injustice of a common condemnation in Adam by means of a common redemption in Christ? At least it appears to be, in effect, the doctrine that all are in principle condemned in Adam while all are in principle redeemed in Christ.[8]

Hodge is the great formative theologian of traditional American Presbyterian theology, occupying a position relatively similar to that of Augustine in relation to Catholic theology, of Calvin in relation to Reformed theology, and of Edwards in relation to New England theology. For all discussion and debate in these various traditions, subsequent to these men, is in relation and reaction to their formulations. This is eminently the case in the debate on original sin among the American Presbyterian theologians. All significant discussion of the issue subsequent to Hodge is in reaction to his treatment of it in the face of the New England and radical New School attack. The theologians who follow him are all attempting to reject the radical New School doctrine without espousing the distinctive position of the Princeton School; indeed, all are deliberately attempting to escape what they feel to be unscriptural, anti-Au-

---

8. See above, pp. 11 f. (Wesley); 24 f. (Smith); 32 ff. (Hodge). See also Hodge, *Theology*, Vol. I, p. 26.

gustinian, Nominalistic, or Arminian implications of that position.

These theologians may be grouped into three basic divisions. The first division includes those who hold to the primacy of the *natural*, as over against the legal or federal, relationship in the explication of our moral solidarity with Adam — namely the Realists. The second includes those who hold to the primacy of neither relationship but rather to the equal importance of both — namely Landis and Dabney. While the third division includes only Murray who holds to the primacy of the *judicial* relationship.

The cry of all the Realists, of whatever style, is: back to Angustine and the Augustinian tradition! We all are really guilty for Adam's sin and not merely nominally and forensically so, in that we were in him morally participant in a common human nature. Thus when Adam sinned, the whole of the race apostatized with the result that there exists in all of us an apostate human nature which is itself sinful and not the mere occasion for sin. This sin of nature attaches to every person individualized from it so as to render each worthy of condemnation. It is only on this hypothesis of an original sin on the part of generic human nature that each individual can be found really responsible, and thus punishable, for the sin of Adam. This natural union is, from the moral standpoint, the primary one; and though enveloped in mystery, when once granted, it solves all other problems relating to the doctrine of original sin. The federal relationship is strictly secondary and dependent upon it, whether as resulting from a separate declarative act of God (Shedd), or as concreated in the union of nature (Baird). Moreover, any legal solidarity, such as the federal arrangement, which was not inherent in the nature of things, would be arbitrary and unjust. Accordingly, it is evident that, on this scheme, *natural* not legal, union is primary in explaining our moral solidarity with Adam.

The father of this approach in the Presbyterian Church was W.G.T. Shedd who espoused philosophical Realism in its classic form; and as far as the legal relationship with Adam is concerned, came to deny representative union as incompatible with the natural union. Samuel Baird took a more exegetical approach than Shedd, disclaiming philosophical Realism. But his version of the Biblical realism of the Augustinian tradition virtually amounts to philosophical Realism. James H. Thornwell began with the position of Hodge, but in attempting to face the question as to how the covenant arrangement could be just was driven to postulate the distinctive hallmark of Realism, namely, a "generic unity of human nature" distinct from, and in addition to, seminal union of nature. In this connection, we should mention that Henry B. Smith really falls within the pale of philosophical Realism, in that he explicitly claims to hold to a moderate Realism. R. W. Landis also explicitly calls himself a realist in that he holds to a real moral participation of the race in Adam's first sin. But he disclaims any dependence upon philosophical Realism in the elucidation of that moral participation, but rather distinguishes between philosophical Realism on the one hand and the Biblical realism of Augustine and traditional Reformed theology on the other — which, he maintains, is agnostic on the precise mode of our "moral identity" with Adam.

Furthermore, it is the distinctive position of Landis, following R. J. Breckinridge, that, while this moral union is both natural and legal (or federal), neither one of these two aspects of the union is prior to the other. The natural connection and the legal connection are not to be confused or separated; *inherent* (natural) sin and *imputed* (legal) sin are mutually necessary and equally important in the explication of our moral solidarity with Adam, in so far as that union can be explained.

It would appear that R. L. Dabney, while decidedly eclectic in his doctrine, also holds, fundamentally, to this position. Natural depravity and legal guilt must be taken together in the explication of the doctrine of original sin. It is for this reason that the validity of the distinction between mediate and immediate imputation must be strenuously denied. Dabney does maintain, however, that while depravity and guilt are chronologically simultaneous both in Adam's first sin and in the original sin of the race, it is obvious that, from the logical standpoint, depravity of nature is prior to legal guilt.[9]

Professor Murray on the other hand holds, with Hodge, to the priority of the forensic in the explication of our interest in Adam's sin. While with respect to Adam depravity may be logically prior to guilt, with respect to the race judicial guilt is prior to depravity of nature. Depravity of nature devolves upon men by virtue of their special legal

---

9. Such a sentiment might lead one to believe that Dabney holds to the priority of the *natural* relationship. On the other hand, the fact that he agrees with Hodge that the object of the imputation is judicial liability alone would lean in the opposite direction toward the priority of the *legal* relationship. Obviously, Dabney's position is not unified and self-consistent.

solidarity, however one designates it, with Adam. It is inherent in the very nature of the sin imputed to them on the basis of this legal solidarity so that, contrary to Hodge, we are really culpable for Adam's sin. The legal relationship is prior to the natural; the natural is under the aegis of the legal.

So much for the interpretative historical summary; it is now necessary to analyze and evaluate the various viewpoints from a more theological perspective. After all, the question naturally arises: which of the contending views is the right one? Now in attempting to face this question, it is not our intent to formulate our own approach to the problem of original sin. Nor shall we attempt to argue for the validity of any one of the proposed solutions in its entirety, but rather submit in summary form certain critical judgments which may contribute toward the appreciation of the past and the formulation of the future. In doing so, it would be profitable to arrange these remarks in terms of the various areas of issue in the debate — namely, what may be designated the *historical* issue, the *epistemological* issue, the *exegetical* issue, and finally the more strictly *theological* issue.

We must, however, preface such an analysis with certain pertinent observations. At the outset of such analysis, we might be tempted to pass off the whole debate as irrelevant to theological "truth" in that it starts with a hopelessly antiquated problematic. Such would be the summary evaluation of "modern" theology with its denial of the truthfulness of scripture — indeed, of the very existence of truth itself — in any traditionally orthodox sense. The anti-intellectualism of modern theology would deny that there is any problem of original sin in the sense in which the historic Christian church has grappled with that problem.[10] But this is an easy-way-out approach. It is typical of the easy-way-out approach of modern theology in general, which in refusing to face up to the real theological problems posed by a genuine divine revelation, sinks itself into the far more disturbing problems lurking in the mire of agnosticism. It would be theological suicide for the Church to take the

---

10. See, e.g., Rudolf Bultmann's famous essay on demythologization: "Human beings are subject to death even before they have committed any sin. And to attribute human mortality to the fall of Adam is sheer nonsense, for guilt implies personal responsibility, and the idea of original sin as an inherited infection is sub-ethical, irrational, and absurd" — *Kerygma and Myth,* New York, 1961, p. 7.

modernistic short-cut and deny historic Christianity in the process.

In much the same vein, we would maintain that the Presbyterian theologians were right in rejecting the revived Pelagianism of the radical New School theology as not only unscriptural but also as a denial of the whole problem of original sin. They considered the typical New England doctrine in much the same light as Augustine considered Pelagianism as an easy way out at a frightful cost.

Now with regard to the *historical* issue involved in the Presbyterian debate, all the theologians involved appealed in some way to traditional Reformed theology for support. But, as has been demonstrated above, the very ambiguity of that tradition precluded any conclusive appeal to the traditional theology of the Reformed and Presbyterian Churches. On this score, while all participants in the debate could find some semblance of support in classic Reformed theology, none was able to prove conclusively that his distinctive formulation was *the* traditional Reformed doctrine. In this connection, it would appear from the evidence that, in so far as one could manufacture any broad consensus of opinion in the theological tradition of the Reformed Churches, Hodge was farthest from that consensus and Landis closest to it.

But then, as all would admit, the issue ultimately has to be decided on exegetical grounds. It is evident, however, from the course of the debate, that right at this point an *epistemological* issue is raised; that is, the issue as to what the scriptures can, or cannot, be interpreted to teach as to the truth, especially moral truth. The issue may also be called a hermeneutical one; and, as can be readily observed, is an ethical issue as well.

This issue boils down to whether we derive our ultimate epistemological presuppositions from special revelation, or not. For instance, while we may derive the formal concepts of "possibility" and "justice" from revelation in our own consciousness, is the material content of these concepts, taken in its totality, ultimately derived from scripture, or not? It is evident that the latter is not the case with the Pelagian, Nominalist, and New England approaches to the doctrine of original sin. Nor would it seem that such was the case with Hodge and Dabney. On their presuppositions, it were both impossible and unjust for us to have been involved in any real participation in Adam's sin beyond that of a merely forensic nature. Thus the content of their concepts of what is possible and what is just seems to be ultimately derived from what they would consider the common sense intuitions of the intellectual and moral consciousness of man. Though to be fair to these men, we should have to add that they would maintain that there is scriptural warrant for following this procedure — that is, there is warrant in special revelation for so appropriating the content of natural revelation.

At any rate, it would be safer for us always to make the self-conscious attempt to derive the ultimate content of our notions of possibility and impossibility, right and wrong, and the like, from scripture alone — which is more easily said than done. A prime example of this difficulty is Landis, who boldly declares that if God has revealed that we all have sinned in that one sin of Adam, then that settles the matter regardless of whether we can understand how this is possible or just. But at the same time, as Dabney well points out, he falls into the inconsistency of castigating the distinctive exegesis of Hodge on the ground that scripture cannot teach what is an affront to the universal moral consciousness of the race. The great danger in this approach is that we shall distort scripture by *detracting* from the comprehensive totality of its message as the whole counsel of God.

There is, on the other hand, the great danger of weakening and thus in a measure distorting, the scriptural revelation by *adding* to it by means of philosophical speculation. This is specifically the danger involved in the rationalist Realism of Shedd and the empiricist Nominalism of Edwards. These men attempt to explain the possibility and justice of what seems to be the plain teaching of scripture by appeal to extra-scriptural philosophical speculation — speculation which, on its ultimate presuppositions, may very well be not only extra-scriptural, but on that very account also ultimately anti-scriptural.

In this connection, it would only be fair to recognize that both Edwards and Shedd desire to be true to the content of plain scriptural teaching resulting from historical exegesis. It is only for the apologetic purpose of defending this teaching to the world that they indulge in their speculations. Their speculation is the result of their response to the critics of the possibility of the scriptural doctrine's being true. Moreover, we must recognize that it is one thing to derive the content of one's doctrine from extra-scriptural sources, and quite another to attempt to express scriptural content in extra-scriptural forms of thought — though we must ever be on guard that extra-scriptural thought forms do not lead us to anti-scriptural thought content.

We should also note that the charge of adding to scripture may also be leveled at certain aspects of classic covenant theology. For just as Edwards and Shedd were dependent on certain philosophical leanings for the restatement and defense of scriptural truth, much of covenant theology was dependent on certain extra-scriptural legal ideas prevalent in the seventeenth century, ideas which may very well have been used to the distortion of the covenant theology of scripture. For just as Edwards and Shedd have gone beyond the strictly scriptural account of our *natural* solidarity with Adam as consisting in seminal union, many of the covenant theologians may have gone beyond the strictly scriptural account of our *legal* solidarity with the head of the race.

The former observations lead us directly to the strictly *exegetical* issue involved in the debate. All of the basic theological positions were represented by men who were capable exegetes of scripture. Even Albert Barnes was no mean exegete; it was simply that on this point his exegesis was corrupted by his unscriptural theological presuppositions. And we may conclude that, from the strictly exegetical standpoint, Professor Murray's exegesis is the most painstaking and thorough, the least vitiated by unhealthy presuppositions, and therefore the soundest.

This does not mean, however, that Murray's exegesis of Romans 5:12 ff., and the theological formulation based upon it, is without its problems. For instance, there is the question: In what sense did all sin in Adam's first sin? Murray accepts the reality of universal sin, and thus culpability, in the first sin, but, in the end, ultimately explains this sin and culpability in forensic categories. But can the reality of this universal act of sin be exhausted by explanation in merely forensic terms? Again, there is the question of just how far can one push the obvious parallelism between condemnation through Adam and justification through Christ in the interpretation of Romans 5?

These two basic exegetical questions which have just been raised are obviously closely intertwined and lead directly to the consideration of the more strictly *theological* issue in the debate. It is right in this area of the relationship of the doctrine of original sin to other doctrines that Murray's formulation has to face real problems.

Murray is right, in response to previous criticism of Hodge's view, in rejecting the latter's notion of an exact parallel between Christ's bearing the guilt of our sins and our bearing the guilt of Adam's sin. He is also right in rejecting the Wesleyan version of the parallelism between condemnation in Adam and justification in Christ. But, in this very connection, how can he, with his distinctively Princeton view of the nature of the parallelism between the two, escape an essentially Arminian view of justification on the one hand or the doctrine of eternal justification on the other? In other words, Murray has given no answer to this very criticism which was leveled at Hodge by Landis and Dabney in the course of the nineteenth century debate.[11]

Again, one might ask whether Murray's modification of Hodge's position allows him to escape, in terms of his formulations, that very mediate imputation which he so strenuously denies. For if depravity of nature is by definition contained in the nature of the sin of Adam imputed to posterity, does this not imply that the imputation of the guilt of that sin is ultimately mediated by a prior participation in its depravity? And in response to the pressure of this implication, can one make such a sharp distinction between the nature of the imputation on the one hand and the nature of the sin imputed on the other?[12]

At any rate, even if this sharp distinction will hold, another problem pushes itself to the fore, and that is just this: How can depravity of nature be imputed? If imputation is a divine operation solely in the sphere of the forensic, how can depravity, a matter which concerns the actual moral state of one's human nature, be the object of a forensic judgment? Is not imputation solely concerned with one's legal standing, and not with the moral state of one's nature; so that while we may speak of the imputation of sin's guilt, including genuine culpability, we may not speak of the imputation of sin's pollution? Or may we speak not only of the imputation of forensic categories such as guilt and righteousness, but also of natural (that is, natural in the sense of referring to the actual moral state of human nature) categories such as moral pollution and ethical righteousness? In other words, can the categories of the legal and natural spheres, due to the fact of their empirically close relationship, be so confused?

These questions lead us back to the fundamental question as to how we are to relate the legal and natural (in the sense used above) aspects of our sinful relationship to Adam. Now, as we take a final look at the theological problems raised in debate, we may ask a similar question as to the nature of our saving relationship to Christ. And then

---

11. See above, pp. 74 f. (Landis); 83 f. (Dabney).

12. The sharpness of this distinction was the essence of the answer of Professor Murray when the author pressed him with the above implication in November of 1966.

we may also, in the light of the scriptural parallelism between sinfulness in Adam and salvation in Christ, inquire further into the nature of this parallelism.

There is no salvation in scripture apart from solidarity with Christ the Mediator and Redeemer. What then is the full significance of this solidarity? In other words, what does the expression "in Christ" really mean?

It is evident, first of all, that there is a *legal* aspect of union with Christ. The saved are judicially in Christ and as such are recipients of the blessing of justification, that is, salvation from the condemning sanctions of the law, or the legal aspect of salvation.

There is also at the same time what is commonly called a mystical aspect of union with Christ. Those who are participant in the redemption that is in Christ Jesus are mystically one with Christ. Whatever may be the precise nature of this mystical solidarity, it has three phases in human experience: first, an *initial* phase commonly called regeneration in traditional Reformed theology;[13] second, a *continuing* phase commonly called progressive sanctification; and, third, a *final* phase commonly called glorification, that is, the consummation of our mystical union with Christ when we shall see Him face to face. The question naturally arises as to the precise nature of this mystical union and its relationship to the legal union.

The foregoing account, however, by no means exhausts the fullness of the scriptural significance of solidarity with Christ. For we find in scripture that there is much more than this experiential aspect of union with Christ. There is also an historical aspect, and indeed an eternal aspect. For all the redeemed are not only to be saved by being *experientially* in Christ, but they were also in some sense *historically* in Him when He lived, died, rose again, and ascended on high; they were all redeemed in Him in history. And not only so, but every last one of them is elect *eternally* in Him before the foundation of the world. Given these awesome disclosures of divine revelation, the question naturally arises: What precisely is the nature of these three aspects? What is the precise relationship between them? And how do they relate to the dis-

---

13. It is here recognized that the term "regeneration" has not always been used in this restricted sense in Reformed theology, but that in the earliest Reformed theology it was applied to all three phases of the renewal of one's moral nature, not simply the initial one.

tinction between the legal and mystical aspects of solidarity with Christ?

Now if we may reason from the nature of saving solidarity with the last Adam to the nature of sinful solidarity with the first Adam, we may compare the moral relationship to Adam with the moral relationship to Christ. In doing so, we may compare the *legal* union with Adam to the legal union with Christ and ask in what sense condemnation in Adam is analogous to justification in Christ. We may also compare the natural union with Adam to the mystical union with Christ, or what may be called the *vital* union with the former to the vital union with the latter. Now we know that whereas the vital union with Adam is natural, the vital union with Christ is supernatural; but may we not ask whether there is perhaps a divinely intended analogy between these two relationships, and, if so, what is the precise nature of such an analogy?

Following along with this line of inquiry, we may ask whether there is any legitimate analogy between the various phases of the vital, or mystical, union with Christ and what might be corresponding phases of the vital union with Adam. For instance, is there any divinely intended analogy between the initial phase of the vital union with Christ, namely supernatural *regeneration* in righteousness, and the initial phase of the vital union with Adam, namely natural *generation* in sin? And is there a continuing phase of the vital union with the first Adam, some sort of progressive degradation or pollution, to correspond to progressive sanctification in the second Adam?

Next we may inquire into the overall relationship between *vital* union on the one hand and *legal* union on the other, whether with reference to solidarity with Adam or with Christ. Does the vital determine the legal, or the legal the vital, or are both mutually and equally determinative in explicating the nature of one's moral solidarity with Adam or with Christ? Is the vital prior to the legal, or the legal to the vital, or is neither one prior to the other? And if there be any such priority or primacy, is it a logical or a chronological priority; or both, depending on the specific phase of the solidarity? Or would such priority depend upon whether it was in reference to moral solidarity with Adam or with Christ? For instance, if on the one hand the initial phase of mystical union with Christ, namely regeneration, is at least logically prior to justification, may not justification on the other hand be both logically and chronologically prior to the continuing phase of the mystical union, namely progressive sanctification? Also, would this same scheme hold in exactly parallel fashion in the explication of the relationship between the vital and legal aspects of moral solidarity with Adam? That is, is there an initial depravity of nature which is logically prior to original guilt and the resultant condemnation? And is this condemnation logically and chronologically prior to a progressive degradation leading to a final and irreparable moral depravity?

Finally, we may inquire into whether there is any proper analogy between the eternal, historical, and experiential aspects of union with Christ and similar aspects of union with Adam? That is, is there a three-fold eternal, historical, and empirical union with Adam to correspond to the analogous threefold union with Christ? For instance, were we all polluted and condemned in Adam before the foundation of the world in the eternal purpose of God? And was this purpose carried out in the historical fall of the race in Adam? Now since Adam both sinned as an individual and as the race, we all sinned in him. But did we sin in him vitally or legally, or both — whether legally because vitally, or vitally because legally, or vitally and legally in one common moral act? And how is this sin communicated to us at the inception of our empirical solidarity with Adam at birth — legally because vitally, or vitally be-cause legally, or without the logical or temporal priority of either? That is, by legal imputation because of the vital (natural) propagation, or by vital propagation because of legal imputation, or by imputation and propagation mutually operative and equally determinative? And finally, did we sin in Adam and is his sin communicated to us as a race or as individuals? That is, are we guilty of that sin as a race or as individuals? Or is there no difference between racial and individual guilt?

It is hoped that the foregoing account of the theological ques-tions raised by the debate on the problem of original sin in American Presbyterian theology may be both an incentive and guideline for further exegetical research.[14] In the meantime, we have a reliable and glorious doctrine of original sin to teach and preach to sinful men. It is reliable because it was given to us by Christ Himself through His holy prophets and apostles of old; and it is glorious because, by the disclosure of the

---

14. There has recently appeared a significant exegetical contribution in this area: R.P. Shedd, *Man in Community* (A Study of St. Paul's Application of Old Testament and Early Jewish Conceptions of Human Solidarity), Grand Rapids, 1964. Dr. Shedd's study, however, seems to lack insight into the nature of the theological problems outlined above. Moreover, his treatment of the data of Rom. 5 is not thorough, nor does he take account of Professor Murray's exegesis of that passage.

need of salvation and by the force of analogy, it magnifies the work of the Savior. And this is true whether we can answer, or even understand, all the questions related to the details of the doctrine. In this connection we must realize that, from the nature of the case, we shall never have all the answers to those questions which arise from our attempt to understand divine revelation in relation to that world of thought and phenomena in which we find ourselves. Nevertheless, such a realization ought not and must not preclude the painstaking exegesis of scripture with a view to the precise formulation of the doctrines of Christ. In the meantime we may know, and rest in the knowledge, that God Almighty and Eternal is the final Arbiter of what is possible and just; and that He is thus good in terms of the highest possible concept of goodness. It may very well be that the more we derive our essential problematic from the Bible itself, and the more we present this Biblical problematic to others, the less problem we and they may have with the doctrine of original sin.

Above all, and at all costs, we must beware of, and avoid becoming, problem-centered in all our thinking, teaching, and preaching with regard to the doctrine of original sin. And this is only possible because the sickeningly interrogative mood of our hearts has been transformed into the joy of a new mood — indicative, exclamatory, and imperative — all by means of this simple gospel: namely, that just as we may know that we were ruined in Adam, so we may *know* that we were redeemed in Christ — as we cling to Him with all our hearts!

Bibliography

I. Primary Literature

Augustine, St. A., *Anti-Pelagian Writings* (Nicene and Post-Nicene Fathers, ed. Philip Schaff, Vol. V), New York: The Christian Literature Company, 1887.

___ (J.P. Migue, ed.), *Patrologiæ Latinæ*, Tomus XLV, Paris, 1865.

Baird, S.J., *The Elohim Revealed in the Creation and Redemption of Man*, Philadelphia: Parry & McMillan, 1860.

Bellamy, Joseph, *Works*, Boston: Doctrinal Tract and Book Society, 1850.

Breckinridge, R.J., *The Knowledge of God, Objectively Considered*, New York: Robert Carter and Brothers, 1858.

Calvin, John, *Institutes of the Christian Religion* (tr. Henry Beveridge), Vols. I and II, Grand Rapids: Eerdmans, 1957.

_____, *Institutio Christianæ Religionis*, Vol. I (ed. A. Tholuck), Edinburgh: T. & T. Clark, 1874.

Dabney, Robert L., *Discussions*, Vol. I, Evangelical and Theological, Richmond: Presbyterian Committee of Publication, 1890.

_____, *Systematic and Polemic Theology*, Richmond: Presbyterian Committee of Publication, 1927.

Fairbairn, Patrick (ed.), *Princeton Theological Essays*, Edinburgh: T. & T. Clark, 1856.

Edwards, Jonathan, *Works*, Vol. I (10th ed.), London: Henry G. Bohn, 1865.

Emmons, Nathanael, *Works*, Vol. IV, Boston: Crocker & Brewster, 1842.

Hodge, A.A., *The Atonement* (ed. W.H. Goold), London: T. Nelson and Sons, 1868.

_____, *Outlines of Theology*, London: T. Nelson and Sons, 1879.

Hodge, Charles, *Commentary on the Epistle to the Romans* (rev. ed., 1886), Grand Rapids: Eerdman's, 1960.

_____, *Systematic Theology*, Vols. I-III, Grand Rapids: Eerdmans, n.d.

_____(ed.), *The Biblical Repertory and Princeton Review* (For the Year 1860), Philadelphia: Peter Walker, 1860.

Hopkins, Samuel, *Works,* Boston: Doctrinal Tract and Book Society, 1854.

Landis, R. W., *The Doctrine of Original Sin,* Richmond: Whittet & Shepperson, 1884.

Leith, J. H. (ed..), *Creeds of the Churches,* New York: Doubleday, 1963.

Machen, J. Gresham, *The Christian View of Man,* New York: The Macmillan Co., 1937.

Murray, John, *The Imputation of Adam's Sin,* Grand Rapids: Eerdmans, 1959.

_____, *The Epistle to the Romans,* Vol. One (Ch. I-VIII), Grand Rapids: Eerdman's, 1959.

Niemeyer, H.A. (ed.), *Collectio Confessionum in Ecclesiis Reformatis Publicatarum,* Lipsiae: 1840.

Owen, John, *Works* (ed. Wm. H. Goold), Vols. 5 and 10, New York: Carter & Brothers, 1852.

Shedd, W. G. T., A *Critical and Doctrinal Commentary Upon the Epistle of St. Paul to the Romans,* New York: Charles Scribners Sons, 1879.

_____, *Dogmatic Theology,* Vols. I-III, Grand Rapids: Zondervan, n.d.

_____, *Theological Essays,* New York: Scribner, Armstrong & Co., 1877.

Smith, H.B., A *System of Theology* (3rd ed.), New York: Armstrong and Son, 1888.

_____, *A System of Theology* (4th ed.), New York: Armstrong and Son, 1890.

_____, *Faith and Philosophy,* New York: Scribner, Armstrong & Co., 1877.

Stansbury, A.J. (ed.), *Trial of the Rev. Albert Barnes On a Charge of Heresy,* New York: Van Nostrand & Dwight, 1836.

Taylor, N. W., *Concio ad Clerum* (A Sermon Delivered in the Chapel of Yale College, September 10, 1828), New Haven: Hezekiah Howe, 1828.

_____, *Lectures on the Moral Government of God* (2 vols.), New York: Clark, Austin, & Smith, 1859.

Thomas, Aquinas, St., *Summa Theologiæ,* Vol. 26, New York: McGraw-Hill, 1965.

_____, *Summa Theologica*, Vol. 7 (2nd no.), London: Burns, Oates & Washburn, 1915.

Thornwell, James H., *Collected Writings* (ed. J. B. Adger), Vol. I (Theological), Richmond: Presbyterian Committee of Publication, 1871.

Turrettini, François, *Theological Institutes* (Selections from tr. G. M. Giger), Unpublished, produced in mimeographed form by Pittsburgh Theological Seminary.

Turrettino, François, *Institutio Theologiæ Elencticæ*, Amstelodami: Franscisum vander Platts, 1701.

Warfield, Benjamin B., *Studies in Theology*, New York: Oxford University Press, 1932.

Wesley, John, *Works*, Vol. IX (*Original Sin*), London: Wesleyan Methodist Bookroom, n.d.

Woods, Leonard, *Works*, Vols. II-IV, Boston: Congregational Board of Publication, 1854.

II. Secondary Literature

Berkhof, Louis, *Systematic Theology*, Grand Rapids: Eerdmans, 1959.

Cunningham, William, *Historical Theology*, Vol. I, London: The Banner of Truth Trust, 1960.

_____, *The Reformers and the Theology of the Reformation*, Edinburgh: T. & T. Clark, 1892.

Danhof, R. J., *Charles Hodge As a Dogmatician*, Goes (Netherlands): Oosterbaan & Le Cointre, 1929.

Fisher, G. P., *Discussions in History and Theology*, New York: Scribners, 1880.

_____, *History of Christian Doctrine*, Edinburgh: T. & T. Clark, 1896.

Foster, F. H., *A Genetic History of the New England Theology*, Chicago: The University of Chicago Press, 1907.Gross, J., *Geschichte des Erbsündendogmas* (2 vols.), Basel: Reinhardt, 1960, 1963.

Kelly, J. N. D., *Early Christian Doctrines* (2nd ed.), New York: Harper and Row, 1960.

Loetscher, L. A., *The Broadening Church*, Philadelphia: The University of Pennsylvania Press, 1954.

Oberman, H.A., The *Harvest of Medieval Theology*, Cambridge: Harvard University Press, 1963.Seeberg, R., *Text-Book of the History of Doctrines* (tr. C.E. Hay), Grand Rapids: Baker, 1964.

Shedd, R.P., *Man In Community: A Study of St. Paul's Application of Old Testament and Early Jewish Conceptions of Human Solidarity*, Grand Rapids: Eerdman's, 1964.

Smith, H.S., *Changing Conceptions of Original Sin: A Study in American Theology Since 1750*, New York: Scribners, 1955.

Smith, M.H., *Studies in Southern Presbyterian Theology*, Amsterdam: Van Campen, 1962.

Wiggers, G.F., *Augustinianism and Pelagianism* (tr. Ralph Emerson), Andover: Gould, Newman, and Saxton, 1840.

www.ingramcontent.com/pod-product-compliance
Lightning Source LLC
LaVergne TN
LVHW022323080426
835508LV00041B/2168